C O N T E N T S

PAGE

CONTENTS

INTRODUCTION

The aim of this pamphlet is to introduce, guide and support teachers through a particular approach to the teaching of history. It is our firm conviction that drama techniques, and in particular drama role play, can be used in the classroom to deepen and extend children's understanding of the past to an extent that a study of historical evidence alone will fail to achieve. History through Drama is not a substitute for the skills of the historian - the interpretation of the historical record; rather it seeks to work alongside these techniques to offer a deeper insight into past lives.

Any approach requires support in the early stages, either in the form of personal involvement, or through making techniques accessible in other forms. Although there are many accounts of individual projects, there is no single, up-to-date guide which draws together descriptive accounts with general advice on how to implement the approach in a teacher's own school. The work of Fines and Verrier which encouraged many teachers to examine the use of drama techniques in the teaching of history is now, sadly, long out of print.[1] This pamphlet aims to meet the need for a new publication which builds on recent developments in classroom practice. It begins by placing the contribution of drama in the wider context of history teaching with a discussion of the debate surrounding the empathy issue. The following sections deal specifically with the practical implications of adopting a History through Drama approach in the classroom, from the earliest stages of role play to the organisation of an (optional!) whole day's event. A particular feature is the inclusion of a separate, though closely related section, dealing in more detail with the drama techniques considered in the text. At every stage ideas are informed by extensive practical examples drawn from our own work in schools. Finally our contributors reflect the variety of approaches that History through Drama generates.

The pamphlet is directed towards teachers working in the upper primary age range, ie. with children from eight to twelve years. This is because this is the area in which much of our own personal experience lies and from which our examples are largely drawn. The methods we shall describe are also well-suited to the more flexible timetable found in many primary and middle schools, with their emphasis on cross-curricular work. However, we are confident that many of the strategies are applicable to both younger and older children and this is supported by the experiences of both ourselves and our contributors. We have involved first schools in our projects with great success, while Alan Dennis and Ray Verrier describe their approach in a secondary school with its more rigid timetable. The adaptability of History through Drama is further strengthened by Mike Corbishley's account of an English Heritage project involving special schools. History through Drama is both active and practical; it involves children in 'doing things' rather than being the passive recipients of information. It is child-centred in that it draws on the children's own experiences, and then attempts to lead them outwards into new situations and encounters. And finally it is truly cross-curricular as the need to find out more builds on the contribution of other subject areas.

PART 1: DEFINITIONS

The use of drama in teaching history is not new and we would certainly make no claims for originality. It is a good example of a method which has grown from the grassroots level of the classroom in an attempt to make history more accessible to young children. This has been supplemented by a growing awareness within the supporting services, such as museums education units and the custodians of historic sites, of the potential drama offers for making collections of artefacts and monuments more meaningful. English Heritage, as one of our contributors shows, and the National Trust are now regularly involved in Living History events, while specialist centres such as Clarke Hall in Wakefield show how some historic houses are using role-play as part of their educational programmes.[2] Added to the increasing body of published material are the many projects which are never committed to paper, but show the growing enthusiasm for this approach.

Within these many examples there will be as many possible interpretations of what History through Drama really is. In arriving at our own definition it is simpler to consider initially what we would NOT include. This is not to suggest that the rest of the pamphlet will be negative or dismissive of other viewpoints, but to eliminate certain basic misconceptions which have often dogged our work. History through Drama is NOT about pageants or plays: there are no scripts and no audience. The drama arises spontaneously, but from a structured framework of which history is the foundation. Neither are there any observers: adults, and this may include parents as well as teachers, take part in the drama equally alongside the children in a shared experience. And finally, because we have frequently heard the comment levelled at ourselves, (and by those who should really know better!), History through Drama is NOT 'any excuse to dress up'. Costume may at times have a necessary part to play, but it is always an accessory to, rather than the focal point of, the action.

In comparison we believe that what we have to offer is a much richer and more worthwhile learning experience, and one that brings as its rewards the interest, enthusiasm and motivation of the children involved. The approach is centred on certain basic principles which we define as the 'three Key Elements' of our work. The Key Elements comprise:

1. Detailed investigation into a chosen period, based on the available evidence. This provides the context and framework for:

2. The development of a 'personal history' through drama role play which is consistent with the historical evidence.

3. As the culmination of the project, an entire day spent in role at, wherever possible, an authentic historic site.

In order to achieve all three elements, we would ask teachers considering this approach to allow for several weeks (we recommend at least half a term) of classroom work.

Although we see the three Key Elements of research, role creation and a day on site as closely linked, this may seem too ambitious for teachers embarking on such a project for the first time, especially if they are working alone, or without the support network of an LEA advisory service or local College. Nevertheless, we feel that many of the techniques we shall be describing can be readily absorbed into daily classroom work and need not require the sort of time commitment we have suggested earlier. For this reason we describe the aspects of background research leading towards the personal history separately, so teachers can build upon them in the classroom without the necessity of working towards an entire day's role play. In addition, Alan Dennis and Ray Verrier describe a classroom-based approach in some detail (see pp. 55-60).

Any consideration of teaching methods at this present time must take into account the demands of the National Curriculum. One of the more positive results of recent legislation may be to raise the profile of history in primary schools, through its role as a foundation subject. The teaching of history at first and middle school level has frequently been criticised for its lack of structure and progression. By making history compulsory for all children, and supporting this with a clearly defined framework, government policy may actively encourage the development of good practice in this subject area.

The significance of History through Drama to developments in the National Curriculum can be perceived at many different levels. In terms of history as a discrete subject, it offers a teaching strategy which is essentially content free. The techniques which we will describe can be related to any historical period or topic, helping to make the abstract nature of the past meaningful and accessible to young children. Through the practical opportunities afforded them by drama role play, children have the opportunity to practice the skills history seeks to develop: in particular the handling and interpretation of evidence. Although no formal evaluation of these methods exists as yet, we are confident that such an enactive approach to history brings children closer to conceptual understanding of the historical process.[3] The importance of an empathetic response to the past is especially significant here.

History through Drama projects also offer an excellent opportunity to develop an integrated approach to the curriculum. DES proposals for the core subjects Maths, English and Science all stress the importance of applying these areas across the curriculum. Schools with which we have worked have explored practical science by experimenting with materials available at previous periods, while the examination of manufacturing methods has provided valuable experience of early technology. The single example of one drama situation - the marketplace - offers the opportunity to develop a wide range of mathematical skills through a comparison of monetary values and coinage systems, together with methods of weighing and measuring. Depending on the period under study, there will be many other similar opportunities.

Furthermore, History through Drama provides a significant contribution to the development of oracy. With Speaking and Listening now recognised as an important element of the English curriculum, and drama itself given prominence in the Cox report, teachers will be looking for further opportunities to develop children's competence in these areas. A History through Drama approach offers a number of contexts for meaningful talk: these would range across the spectrum of language function depending upon the drama situations developed and the use of preparatory activity.

It is beyond the scope of this short publication to consider fully all the cross-curricular implications of our work. In any project in which we have been involved, children have also experienced learning in the areas of art/craft, music, dance, and moral and social education, which has included developing children's awareness of cultural values other than their own. In conclusion we consider that the ideas which we shall explore reflect examples of good primary practice which the National Curriculum is seeking to extend.

PART 2: THE IMPORTANCE OF EMPATHY

Recent trends in history teaching have stressed the importance of activity-based learning in which skills and concepts fundamental to an understanding of the subject are developed. This approach is effectively represented in the DES publication, <u>History in the Primary and Secondary Years.</u>[4] The document, representing official HMI views, places schemes and content of work firmly within the context of conceptual development. In this way, the study of history emerges as a method of inquiry rather than a body of knowledge to be assimilated.

The impact of the 'new history' in schools has led to an emphasis on the examination of evidence through introducing primary source material into the classroom. Contemporary documents, illustrations, photographs and artefacts are now widely used to enrich the teaching of history with children from the age of five and upwards.[5] The result has been to encourage children to view the subject more as a matter for interpretation and opinion than a collection of facts. However, there remains the danger that this investigative approach, evidence-based and practically-oriented though it certainly is, can still lead to an over-emphasis on gathering and using information. As a result, we may lose sight of the central premise of history teaching - that history is about people. What is needed is a teaching model which enables a connection to be made between the abstract nature of primary sources and the lives of men and women in the past. We believe that the major value of drama in history teaching is to offer a positive way of meeting this challenge. More specifically, it is through the use of drama to develop the essential historical skill of empathy that this connection can be made more effectively.

The importance of developing empathetic skills in children has recently received considerable attention. It is now one of the national criteria for GCSE, where it is formally assessed and tested.[6] This move has not been without its difficulties; one of the main problems being that of arriving at an acceptable definition.[7] Colloquial expressions, such as 'standing in someone else's shoes', or 'looking through another person's eyes' are helpful in the areas of social and personal education, but are not sufficiently specific for historical purposes. HMI define empathy as:

<u>'the ability to enter into some informed appreciation of the predicaments or points of view of other people in the past.......(which) should be part of the learning of all pupils across the whole age and ability range'.</u>[8]

But perhaps more valuable for the primary teacher is the Schools Council description:

<u>'the capacity to understand another person's behaviour on the basis of</u> one's own experience and behaviour <u>and on the basis of information about the other's situation'.</u>[9] (Emphasis ours).

This definition reflects two features of our own practice: firstly, the development of empathetic understanding drawn from the child's own experience, which is, secondly, supported and extended by detailed information about the past.

However, not all historians would agree on the value of the empathetic response. A recent leader article in response to the new GCSE requirements declared empathetic writing to be _'an inducement to make up history, not to derive it from and test it against evidence'_. It later continued to declare it _'a parody of historical method'_.[10] These misgivings are shared, albeit in a more temperate form, by Jenkins and Brickley, who argue that:

'Just what historical "empathy" is, is a moot point and, whether one can practice it, another. We do not think you can. To us, empathy is a term taken from creative, educational discourses. It is not a term taken from historians and its practice is extremely problematic everywhere'.[11]

This reluctance to accept the term empathy as an integral aspect of historical understanding is reflected by the more recent HMI publication in the Curriculum Matters series.[12] In contrast to their earlier report, History from 5 to 16 does not mention the word empathy at all. However, _'an informed appreciation of the perspectives and motives of people in the past'_ (para. 7) is given as one of the aims of teaching history in schools, and this very closely mirrors HMI's previous definition of empathy. The document goes on to make further suggestions related to their earlier definition: by the age of 11 children should be able to _'make imaginative reconstructions of past situations'_ (para. 9), and that as a principle of teaching and learning history, children _'should have some informed appreciation of the points of view of people living in the past'_ (para. 37).

HMI are quite specific that each of these aspects must take place within the context of the available evidence, and this point is stressed within the three quotations given. The importance of basing imaginative interpretations on the historical record is quite rightly emphasized, as is the danger of _'uncontrolled flights of imagination'_ (para. 11c). This seems to lie at the heart of the hesitancy in using the term empathy - the fact that it may be inconsistent with the work of the historian. However, in our opinion, the HMI criteria are open to much greater abuse than a carefully prescribed definition of empathy which stresses the vital significance of evidence. HMI refer to the ability to make _'imaginative reconstructions'_ (para. 9), and the ability _'to reconstruct historical situations'_ (para. 11c). The problematic word here is 'reconstruct' - a term which is surely inappropriate to the study of history, and one that we would never use in connection with History through Drama. It implies the ability to recreate an event from the past, whereas the historian can, at best, hope to offer only one of several possible interpretations. Therefore it may appear that in a deliberate attempt to avoid a controversial term, HMI have developed criteria which may be open to far more misunderstanding.

In the light of this we would like to offer a working definition of empathy which encompasses the most positive aspects of both the Schools Council and HMI:

'the ability to enter into some informed appreciation of the predicaments or points of view of other people in the past on the basis of one's own experience and behaviour and on the basis of information about the other's situation'.

Within such a definition we would press for acknowledgement of the importance of empathetic skills to historical understanding. Encouraging children to become more aware of alternative viewpoints and experiences seems an essential prerequisite if knowledge of the past is to be something more than information-handling. Such work MUST be carefully structured within the essential framework of the available evidence if it is to be history rather than imagination. In this context, work which enables children to approach more closely the lives of real men and women from the past enhances rather than detracts from the historian's role. Our belief in the significance of empathy to an understanding of history has been one of the strongest motivating forces behind our work in schools. It is a term which we feel is both appropriate and justifiable, and one that we have no hesitation in using.[13]

Empathy in the classroom

There are a number of methods which can be used to develop empathetic skills, so that the contribution of drama needs to be evaluated in the context of a range of strategies available to the teacher.

Simulations present children with structured experiences based on real and fictional historical situations. Children are invited, through the materials provided, to adopt a stance towards an issue under consideration. This could be that of a nineteenth century railway developer,[14] or a philanthropist considering applicants for the position of workhouse matron.[15] Increasingly this is an area where educational software can make a major contribution. Mary Rose[16] and Expedition to Saqqara[17] present pupils with the opportunity to approach the recovery and analysis of evidence from the archaeologist's point of view. In Attack on the Somme[18] participants are required to make strategic decisions as First World War combatants. These are representative of the range of materials available, which utilise the strengths of modern technology in creating successful simulations.

History games, not to be confused with simulations, approach similar issues, but through the medium of a slightly different format. These might be board games, designed to introduce children to the rules of feudal society,[19] or practical problem-solving activities, shown in their best examples on actual historical sites.[20]

However, the value of simulations and games in engendering an empathetic response in children is open to question. Birt and Nichol argue that, through their use, 'the pupils are drawn into a form of understanding and an insight into character and motivation which might otherwise be denied them'.[21] This viewpoint is challenged by Culpin who observed very little of this being achieved through the use of games. In the lessons he describes he found the pupils to be preoccupied with tactics, competitiveness and rules - 'motives and personalities hardly entered into their considerations'.[22] Children have little or no latitude in role creation or definition. The 'characters' are normally presented in a pre-packaged form, with no opportunity for pupils to appreciate how such individuals might have come to hold those particular viewpoints. Unless such simulations are very carefully placed in context, historical understanding is likely to be minimal, and empathy similarly lacking.

Other approaches to empathy build upon the creative response through art or writing. Both of these draw upon the idea of the 'eye-witness' account of a situation. At its worst this can be reduced to a 'Day in the Life of....' style of account, where children are asked to make imaginative leaps from no firm historical foundation. Empathetic writing 'is not an act of untrammelled creative fantasy; it is, at best, a meticulous piece of historical work'.[23] In order to achieve this, the writing has to be consistent with the available evidence, which is in itself the main source of inspiration. It works best when children are fully prepared through background research, and are encouraged to adopt an individual, rather than a generalist, viewpoint.

For these reasons, it is the use of drama role play that offers the greatest potential for the development of empathy. The effective use of role play depends upon tapping the child's previous experiences and enabling them to be utilised in a fresh context. This technique is well-established within the traditions of modern educational drama, and has been used to further social and moral education, as well as being a valuable aid to character development in fictional situations. For instance, children might take on the characters of various concerned parties considering the best use of a piece of urban waste-land.[24] Or they could be asked to adopt the roles of explorers in a 'lost valley' where knowledge of scientific expeditions is utilised to create a collective fiction.[25] In situations such as these, although the children's appreciation of the real-life contexts may be limited, they are able to draw upon some aspects of their previous experience to inform the drama. They will never have taken part in a public hearing, but will have some awareness of the relevance of the availability of play space; they will never have explored the Amazon, but will have had access to both the scientific and the fictional material required for the drama through reading and television.

It is clear that there is a strong link between the requirements for developing historical empathy and drama role play. Both emphasise two key factors for their effectiveness; the contribution of personal experience, and knowledge about a specific context. In historical terms the context is established through the examination of evidence and the use of background reading. This is central to working through drama role play if historical understanding is to be developed. The drama techniques need to continually draw upon the available evidence, to strengthen and deepen the roles the children develop in a way which is consistent with their knowledge about the past. Without this constant referral to sources, there is a danger of creating an 'historical fiction' which does little more than reinforce limited stereotypes.

In our approach, this use of background research is the first of our Key Elements and takes the form of detailed classroom preparation. Our second Key Element, the 'personal history' is developed through drama role play, on the basis of effective research. We believe that empathy is necessarily an individual response, drawing as it does on previous personal experience. This can be related to a study of the past by developing specific, rather than general, roles. The example of a project based on the Norman Conquest which we describe in more detail later (pp. 41-43) illustrates this approach. Instead of becoming 'a Saxon man or woman', the child develops the specific role of 'Elred' or 'Edith', villein in the village of Bretford. In the process of role development, he/she will come into contact with other members of the community - freemen, slaves and Norman overlords, each with his/her own experiences of life in the eleventh century. The individual rather than generalist approach stresses that the viewpoint of a person from the past is dependent upon both the structure of society and his/her position within it. Such an understanding is crucial in developing historical empathy, which depends upon an awareness of the constraints experienced by people in the past.

The third and final Key Element 'use of an authentic historical location' is designed to develop the empathetic process a stage further by giving children the opportunity for a period of extended role play. While we realise that many teachers may not wish to develop their work to this extent, there are important gains to be made from this aspect of History through Drama. By placing a sequence of events in their contemporary context, whether this be an Iron Age hillfort or an eighteenth century country house, the children are helped to deepen their commitment to their individual roles. Freed from the distractions of twentieth century life, and supported by simple costume and appropriate food and drink, the children can approach more closely the lifestyle of the period under study. Such an event, usually lasting for several hours, also provides an opportunity for children to sustain and therefore develop further the personal identities they have been creating in the classroom.

We must emphasize that History through Drama is not, nor ever can be, a reconstruction of the past. Although HMI draw regularly on this term, we feel that any suggestion that the past can be recreated is misguided and harmful to the process of history. No matter how complete the historical record, it will always remain an impossibility to 'know' the thoughts, feelings and actions of our predecessors. In our work with schools, we are offering only one of many possible interpretations of an historical event. This must be stressed throughout the preparatory work to avoid the danger of children believing that 'this was what it was really like'. Neither do the children 'become' characters from the past: while developing their roles they remain themselves throughout, bringing their own experiences to bear upon an imaginary situation, and viewing the past through the eyes of the present. The interpretation which is developed through the drama is at all times consistent with the historical record, so that the empathetic process depends on the investigation and research carried out in the classroom. However, it is vitally important that the children are encouraged to consider alternative viewpoints rather than to offer them one approach as the definitive version. They must be encouraged to be aware that the events and roles presented in the drama are capable of being construed in many different ways if the empathetic experience is to be historically viable. History through Drama is a pretend, but it is not unrestrained imagination.

PART 3: MAKING A PROJECT WORK

Fig. 1 'Planning a Project' summarises the stages of a History through Drama project with a class, and attempts to demonstrate the relationship between background research and drama role play at class, group and individual level. There is a progression of teaching suggested by the numbered items which we believe to be the most effective sequence for planning activities during a project. By following these suggested guidelines, teachers will move towards establishing the second Key Element in our approach: the personal history. In effect the suggested pattern is a spiral one, with each element re-inforcing and extending the level of understanding gained in other areas at an earlier stage. The culmination of the diagram is our third Key Element: the final History through Drama Day, where children will take their personal histories established in the classroom to an authentic location and sustain them throughout a viable historical 'event'. Teachers wanting to work towards such an event may wish to consider this section alongside Part 5, where the planning, preparation and implementation of a final Day is fully considered. Throughout this section we refer to the use of classroom drama without specifying or explaining particular techniques in detail. In an attempt to offer more guidance, Part 4 describes some teaching strategies which teachers will find useful.

1. Background research: to establish the general context

It is vital to prepare the children for the project in a general sense. For the children to be able to choose their role identities, they need to have a body of knowledge about the period in which the project will be based. The corollary of this is that the teacher will have to make certain 'editorial' choices in terms of choosing a focus for future work. A History through Drama approach endeavours to bring pupils together to share a common experience, and therefore children's choices of role will have to be restricted to the context of a single community, or location, in order for this social exchange to take place in later drama sessions. Thus, although the teacher may eventually wish pupils to have some knowledge about widely varying social contexts, and may include this in his or her general introduction to the period under study, the drama element of the work needs to be fixed within a narrower sphere. Information about other contexts can be introduced into the project as it develops, and as this information becomes relevant to the needs of the class.

However, at this stage we suggest that general background research concentrates on investigating those aspects of the period which will inform children's choice of role, such as the range of social groupings. As part of this preparation the range of evidence on which later, more detailed investigation will be based can be introduced. For example, in our Iron Age project, part of the general introduction was an emphasis on the techniques of the archaeologist and the relative shortcomings of interpreting material remains from a prehistoric period. This provided a firm basis on which to build the

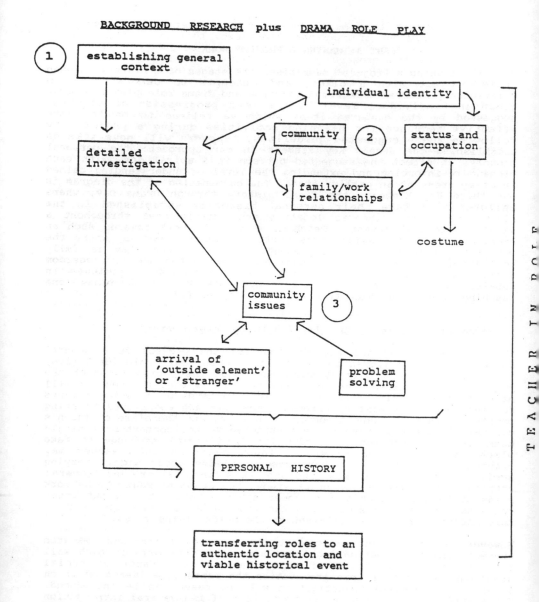

BACKGROUND RESEARCH plus DRAMA ROLE PLAY

① establishing general context

detailed investigation

individual identity

community ②

status and occupation

family/work relationships

costume

community issues ③

arrival of 'outside element' or 'stranger'

problem solving

PERSONAL HISTORY

transferring roles to an authentic location and viable historical event

TEACHER IN ROLE

FIG. 1: PLANNING A PROJECT

16

essential concept that our subsequent interpretation of Iron Age society was only one of many possible views. As a further example, a class working on a medieval project would need to appreciate the role of the Church, the monasteries and the feudal structure, but might approach this learning from the point of view of the inhabitants of a particular village, or from that of the brothers and sisters of a religious foundation. In both cases, the information required could probably be much the same, with a slight variation in emphasis, but the order in which it was acquired would alter, depending on the issues emerging through the drama work. Thus, villagers might find themselves appealing to the monastery or convent for assistance in times of famine, or monks and nuns might find themselves in conflict with the local lord and his villagers with regard to the payment of dues. In either case, general background research will both inform the start of the project, and continue to feed into the developing personal identities and sense of community as the drama role play generates a 'need to know'.

2. Individual identities: promoting personal involvement

On the basis of general background information about the period, the child selects or acquires an 'identity', and the process of empathetic involvement begins. This identity must necessarily be appropriate to the kind of community which has been selected to be the focus of the project, and the name chosen should be authentic wherever possible, both to the period and to the child's status in role. This provides an opportunity for practical research, as names can be taken from documents of the period, gravestones showing appropriate dates, and from contemporary literary sources. A project on Romany life in the early nineteenth century used names taken from the Parish Registers of the villages involved; projects on Victorian school life referred to the admission registers which contained the names of real pupils from a century ago. In cases where events are based on a period before written records, this is less easy. However, there may be references in later literature which can be used, as in the case of the Iron Age project previously mentioned. On the other hand, it may prove an interesting challenge to create fictitious names which seem appropriate to the period. Having determined role names, we and other teachers have found it useful to call the daily class register using these names, both as a re-inforcement for individual pupils, and as a means of familiarising the rest of the class with each other's new identities.

Alongside a name goes the need to give the emerging characters a position in society - indeed in some projects, the selection of status may determine the name attached to the role, or at least narrow the options. Clearly name and status are so closely interdependent that hard and fast rules about which comes first are inappropriate. The decision will have to be made by the teacher in the context of a particular project. However, we do suggest that when considering this early stage of role creation that teachers adopt one general strategy; that all pupils assume the roles of adults. As adults in the project they become part of the decision-making process within the community, rather than being disenfranchised by virtue of age.

It is important to emphasise at this point that girls should not be disadvantaged by the often inferior status afforded them in the past. We take particular care to create roles for girls which are historically viable but which allow for participation in the decision-making processes of the drama. Prehistoric periods offer more possibilities to move away from social stereotypes with the opportunity to create matrilineal cultures with women occupying the prominent social roles. However, in any period of history, it is possible to find examples of women who have status or responsibilities in their own right. At the same time a teacher might wish to concentrate on a predominantly female (or predominantly male) community. This emerged during a project based on a local monastic site, where many of the key historical characters, were monks. In this case it was felt more appropriate to ignore the gender issue, by encouraging girls as well as boys to take on these roles.

In conclusion we would stress that the process of arriving at a name and status for each child is thus carried out within the framework dictated by the context of the community. The following example illustrates the process in operation:

GENERAL CONTEXT: Saxons and Normans.

FOCUS: Britford village in the eleventh century - the locality within which the primary school was situated.

STARTING POINT: Domesday survey of the village, giving information concerning contemporary inhabitants.

KEY QUESTIONS RELATING TO EVIDENCE: How was Domesday Book compiled? Who might be missing from the record? How accurate is the information?

ORGANISATION OF PERSONAL IDENTITIES: Names taken from other contemporary literary sources eg. Anglo-Saxon Chronicle. Status taken from Domesday entry. Class divided into freemen, villeins, cottars and slaves in proportion to those documented in the Survey. Identities arrived at by children drawing first a name then a status from two 'hats'.

REINFORCEMENT: Children draw figures of their new identities and place them on a ladder to show their relative position within the feudal hierarchy. This becomes a constant reference point throughout the project.

TEACHER'S ROLE: Reeve of village - selected so that the teacher can act as an authority figure, but one not too remote.[26]

The Britford project is further developed later in the pamphlet (see pp. 41-43). In this example, working within the framework of a feudal society meant that status was pre-determined by the historical context. For other periods of time community relationships may not be so formally structured. If this is the case, then the occupation of individual characters can be used as an indicator of their relative status. The historical record will often give direct evidence of the types of occupation which took place in certain areas: for the Victorian period, census returns are a most valuable source for this purpose. Where the evidence is incomplete, or even non-existent, occupations can be deduced which are consistent both with the locality and the period under study.

GENERAL CONTEXT: English Civil War.

FOCUS: Conflicting sympathies of Royalist and Parliamentarian supporters.

PRE-REQUISITE CONDITION: Several schools working together on the final day. Reasons needed for inter-action amongst children.

STARTING POINT : Contemporary historical building, with extensive grounds available for use. Strong local connections with period.

ORGANISATION OF PERSONAL IDENTITIES: Names taken from eighteenth century Parish Registers. Family groupings constructed on the basis of 6 members per family, 2 from each of the schools involved. Occupations designated to families, as authentic to period and locality.

REINFORCEMENT: Prior to the final day, schools exchange messages, portraits and letters between family members. Some older children visit their 'relatives' in other schools.

Costume: not just 'dressing up'

A clear indication of status, occupation and period can be given by simple costuming. This can considerably enhance children's involvement in a project at whatever level work is planned. Obviously it is a significant factor if the class is working towards a final full day at an historical location, but there is also a valuable place for the use of costume in wholly classroom-based work. Some teachers are, quite rightly, anxious that History through Drama may involve a considerable outlay of both time and money in getting children 'dressed up', but costume need be neither elaborate nor expensive. Items of clothing which offer the flavour of a particular period while being sufficiently different from modern day dress are all that are required. We would not want any school to be deterred from this

19

approach merely because they felt unable to meet the demands of providing an historical wardrobe for their children.[27] A History through Drama Day which placed a greater emphasis on costume is described in Jo Lawrie's account, although the success of this approach clearly depends on the active co-operation and participation of parents (see p.62).

We would recommend a simple tunic of varying length as a most effective all-purpose, multi-period garment.[28] Worn short over trousers tucked into socks which are cross-gartered, it provides general working men's dress from Prehistoric to Restoration times. Worn long and embellished with a belt and cloak, it may become a noblewoman's gown or a working woman's dress, depending on the fabric and quality of decoration. Shawls, cloaks and hoods made from curtains or blankets quickly create the experience of wearing costume, while successfully hiding modern day clothes underneath.

For teachers working towards a History through Drama Day, it is most important that the children become very familiar with wearing their period clothes well before the final day's activities. As the children deepen their sense of personal identity their costumes should become an integral part of the roles they are developing. Wherever possible we encourage teachers to use costume during the preparatory work in school, so that there are opportunities for children to wear items both during the drama and investigative research sessions. In the Britford Saxons and Normans project, the children themselves chose to wear their costume items in class whenever they were working on this project. At these times they would also only answer to their role names!

Moving into drama: Creating a Community

We have now established the two requisite conditions for drama role play to come into effect. Background research has established the general context of the project. The children have acquired a role name, status and/or occupation, and the beginnings of an awareness of their relationships with other members of their family and community. It is at this point that drama techniques will become a valuable teaching aid, for from now on the children's developing sense of historical identity will be engendered through practical role play operating alongside detailed investigation.

At this stage it is helpful to set targets for the ensuing work. We have presented these as a number of questions, the answers to which will inform the content of the final personal history. The example we have used relates to a topic set in the Iron Age, but each History through Drama project will generate its own set of questions, specific to the period under study. In the process of finding the answers, children will engage in both historical research using primary evidence and secondary sources, as well as interaction with other members of the class through the drama. A series of questions relating to the personal history not only provides a focus for the preparatory work, it is also an invaluable tool for the assessment and evaluation of this teaching strategy. The level of commitment children bring to their roles can be evinced by the quality of their responses to enquiry about their daily lives.

GENERAL CONTEXT: Middle Iron Age

FOCUS: Final History through Drama Day at Danebury Hillfort.

STARTING POINT : Archaeological evidence of the period.

KEY QUESTIONS RELATING TO EVIDENCE : How do we know about communities which leave no written record? What various possible interpretations could we make on the basis of this evidence?

ORGANISATION OF PERSONAL IDENTITIES : Names taken from later Celtic literary sources. Schools become separate tribes, individual classes become clans within tribes. Extended family groupings established within classes. Occupations consistent with evidence chosen by children.

REINFORCEMENT : Oral story telling becomes an important part of transmitting this non-literate culture.

QUESTIONS FOR PERSONAL HISTORY :

1.   What is your name?
2.   What tribe do you belong to, and where is your settlement?
3.   What is your occupation? (This question should create awareness of varying levels of status within each tribal group).
4.   Who are the members of your family?
5.   What clothes do you wear? How are they made?
6.   What does your settlement look like?
7.   What does your home look like - from the outside/inside?
8.   What did you have to eat today? How was it cooked, and how did you eat it?
9.   What do you do when you are not working?
10.   Have you visited any other places? Or can you remember any important events which have taken place in your life?
11.   Do you have any special beliefs/rituals/ceremonies in your tribe?
12.   What are the particular features which give you a tribal identity - ie. do you have some special skill, costume, markings etc. which set you apart from other tribes?
*13.   Why have you come to Danebury today?
*14.   What have you brought with you?
*15.   How did you travel here?

* Questions specifically relating to final History through Drama Day.

NB. These are questions which all adults need to answer as well as children!

For the personal histories to develop from this initial stage, the context of the project has to be enlarged to encompass wider issues. This brings us to the third aspect of our general diagram, the creation of a community which, as it develops, will provide the framework for the emerging role play.

The drama techniques which can be used to provide children with answers to some of the previous questions, and to deepen a sense of their place in a community are varied, but there is one main teaching strategy which underlies a History through Drama project. Role play should be the major teaching method used, as opposed to some form of performance, so that children will experience various events in role as the individuals they have established during their preparatory work.

For this experience to be fully effective, teachers and other adult participants will also need to create and maintain a role identity for themselves. Teaching in role is a hallmark of History through Drama, so that children are both committed to, and comfortable with, their own personal identities, and can also relate easily to the teacher within the context of the drama.

Necessarily, the teacher will have to have decided on the 'location' of the drama work for this to take place. Since each child in the class will have his/her own identity, the location must be such that a number of individuals would normally be expected to live their lives there. This might be, for example, a village, a section of a town (or even an entire town if we accept the existence of other, invisible, townspeople), a manor, a monastery, a Roman villa, or a large country house.

In any case, the geography of the location needs to be established early in the project, to give the children a sense of collective and individual 'place'. This provides an excellent opportunity for the introduction of evidence-based research. If plans or contemporary maps of the location already exist, then work centres upon these. We used such material with considerable success in a project based on Tudor Southampton. A map by John Speed of 1611 gave contemporary information on the geography of the town. The street names provided addresses for all the children involved and formed the basis of class investigation. By comparing their own address and occupation with that of other children, pupils were able to draw conclusions about the types of neighbourhood which might have existed within the city. As a result of this, they became more aware of the concentrations of various related trades and occupations in different quarters. The area near the waterfront revealed an emphasis on work associated with the port, plus a number of taverns, while French Street and English Street were the commercial centre of the city. In this way, primary source material can be used as the foundation of much practical investigative work which both extends and enriches children's sense of personal and collective identity.

The following example shows how name, occupation and location form the basis for a seventeenth century community with a class of 7 to 8 year olds. The source for the children's role names was Southampton parish registers.

Child's name	Role name	Occupation	Address	Age
Stuart Ingram	Lenard Mayly	farm labourer	14 Church St	25
Jane Wheeler	Emma Mayly	farm labourer	14 Church St	50
Paul Merrick	William Hilles	wheelwright	27 Church St	20
Donna Scott	Katherine Hilles	wheelwright's wife	27 Church St	20
James Merrick	Nathaniel Lambole	gamekeeper	18 Church St	30
Gemma Yates	Avis Lambole	gamekeeper's wife	18 Church St	28
Richard Wearn	Andrew Watson	weaver	23 Church St	26
Charlotte Moody	Patience Watson	weaver	23 Church St	32
Colleen Hampton	Barbara Godwine	milkmaid	25 Church St	18
Stephen West	Felix Godwine	apprentice blacksmith	25 Church St	17
Kevin Bright	George Faukins	cobbler	47 Merchant St	44
Emma Broomfield	Mary Faukins	cobbler's wife	47 Merchant St	20
Darren Beer	John Bates	weaver	48 Merchant St	20
Emma Cox	Joan Bates	clothes maker	48 Merchant St	20
Sarah Chant	Sarah Barger	butcher's wife	23 Merchant St	20
Tom Stanton	Arter Barger	butcher	23 Merchant St	21
Spencer Curtis	Samuel Mayres	blacksmith	15 Merchant St	26
Hayley Irvine	Rebecca Mayres	blacksmith's wife	15 Merchant St	20
Paul Omasta	James Waterman	farm labourer	18 Riverside Wy	21
Naomi Jupe	Joanne Waterman	farm labourer	18 Riverside Wy	20
Karla Taylor	Elnor Burley	baker	47 Riverside Wy	20
Ian Loveland	Joseph Burley	baker	47 Riverside Wy	22
Helen Mansbridge	Margaret Woldrige	milkmaid	32 Riverside Wy	20
Leanne De Abreu	Esther Woldrige	barmaid	32 Riverside Wy	25
Jodi Yates	Dina Yetman	milkmaid	16 King St	20
Kerry Alford	Susanna Yetman	milkmaid	16 King St	20
Kerry Robinson	Sara Hardinge	farm labourer	17 King St	21
Paul Murphy	Anthony Hardinge	carpenter	17 King St	26
Gavin Wheeler	Jacob Wake	servant	25 King St	20
Lisa Woodman	Avared Wake	weaver	25 King St	20
Kelly Mintram	Anne Nutt	clothes maker	21 King St	18
Kasia Ozmin	Mary Nutt	clothes maker	21 King St	19

Acknowledgement: Charles Savage, Townhill First School, Southampton.

The earliest stages of drama role play concentrate on the individual in his/her family or work group, but quickly extend outwards to interact with the rest of the community. Throughout the preparatory work, it is a good idea to present children with issues which will provide the focus for their work and offer direct experience of the constraints which operated on societies in the past. What follows are a few guidelines which may help teachers in their planning. Problems and issues are grouped together under common strands, and suggestions of practical drama activities included.

Problems and Issues

Many of these issues can be introduced to the class in several different ways. Teachers may like to consider the different effects upon the development of the work which might result from these various types of dissemination.

DISPUTE:
workers' rights in industrial and
    agricultural settings;
women's rights;
tithes, taxes, rent;
boundary and/or water rights;
legal disputes;
mis-use of authority;

THREAT TO COMMUNITY:
famine, drought;
sickness, plague;
invasion, conquest, colonial rule;
eviction, enclosure;
new invention, loss of livelihood;
factory closure or reduction of workforce;
unemployment, lockout;
loss of privileges;

WARFARE:
invasion, conquest;
battle, death;
recruitment, press-gang;

THEFT:
of individual/collective property;
as result of hardship;
punishment of;

JUSTICE:
formal/informal;
judicial systems - clergy/laity;
witness system;
forms of punishment;
justice and privilege;

TRADE:
exchange of goods and relative values;
borders and boundaries;
weights and measures;
quality of merchandise.

These problems and issues need to be introduced into the drama in a way which is both believable and appropriate to the period under consideration. They might include:

> *letters or messages received by the teacher in role or a child in an appropriate role;
> *a poster or a placard 'appears' in a public place;
> *a newspaper article;
> *a photograph;
> public announcement by town crier, important figure, media;
> gossip initiated by teacher in role;
> arrival of a stranger with news or a message.

* These may be based on authentic historical material, or made by the teacher.

Some of the above will be more appropriately introduced through small group work, while others will be best used with the whole class. Each method will probably be used at various times throughout the project, both having their own particular contribution to make so that one should not be seen as a progression from the other. Nevertheless we would suggest that a useful starting point for the drama is to begin with groups centred on the family or workplace.

FAMILY GROUP: activities here might include:

> -getting up in the morning and starting the day;
> -family meal times (possibly discussing work tasks);
> -domestic work in house/garden
> -preparing for visitors/ family celebrations;
> -discussion of problems/issues which affect family;
> -preparing for an event relating to the whole community -
>   (see later examples of whole class work).

WORK GROUPS: these might be virtually identical with family groups in some periods, but might be completely different in others:

> -mimed working activity;
> -discussion of problems/issues associated with workplace;
> -discussion of problems/issues affecting community at large.

There may be many stages throughout the project at which the teacher feels it desirable to ask children to meet in smaller groups in order for discussion to take place which will involve every pupil. The introduction of problems or issues which act as a focus for discussion might be via a larger, whole class activity, or by direct input into a group from the teacher. The following are some examples of situations which can be used when working with the entire class or with larger numbers of children. All provide opportunities for the introduction of new information and the dissemination of knowledge or ideas. Most of these situations could also be incorporated into a programme for a final History through Drama Day.This earlier experience may well help children to feel secure within the context of the larger event.

MARKET PLACE: family/work groups bring produce (mimed or imaginary) for buying and selling activities.

Opportunities for: barter, or using contemporary coinage vocabulary; meeting and talking to other children in role; disputes, eg. short- weight, short changing, rotten produce, sour beer, pick-pocketing etc.

WORK SITUATIONS: particularly suitable if larger numbers of pupils involved (eg. cotton mill, factory).

Opportunities for: collectively mimed working actions; workplace conflict with other workers or employer; exchange of news/gossip about work events or community issues.

INFORMAL SOCIAL EVENTS: such as celebrations, village/tribal gatherings of a social rather than formal nature.

Opportunities for: recounting significant events of the day (or previous period of time); sharing memories of events from the past; telling episodes from communal history; recounting myths/legends; appearance of stranger with message/problem for community; senior member(s) of community to raise issues/problems for more formal debate at a subsequent meeting; informal entertainments (i.e communal singing or dancing).

RITUAL: incorporating religious events, rites of passage (birth, death, initiation, marriage, coming of age), formal celebrations of significance to the community, transfer of power and status (eg. investiture of monarch).

Opportunities for: formalised movements/ritual actions; ritual music, dance and song; re-telling (re-enacting?) significant events in communal past; giving witness - formally acknowledging personal qualities of deceased; development of a formal language register; creation of specific ritual forms.

FORMAL SOCIAL EVENTS: such as court hearings, village/tribal councils. Also may overlap with aspects of ritual (above).

Opportunities for: giving witness;
                          pursuing a reasoned argument within a debate;
                          organising a debate - perhaps with its own
                             recognition of the right to speak;
                          formal entertainments (i.e possible performances).

One means whereby community issues and/or problems can be introduced or polarised is by the introduction of an outside element - the 'stranger'. This role might be taken either by the class teacher, if appropriate, or by a visitor to the class, such as a drama advisory teacher, another member of staff in the school etc. The 'stranger' can bring unexpected news, request help and advice, or challenge the established order and routines of the community. This strategy gives children the opportunity to articulate the knowledge they are gaining by having to explain their circumstances to the newcomer. As a result they may have to re-evaluate the central issues or tenets of community life which they have devised in their previous work.

Examples

CONTEXT: Medieval villages project.

PROBLEM: Local dispute over state of repair of tidal causeway, and cost of toll for causeway use.

SOURCE: Contemporary lease relating to Eling Tide Mill.

TEACHER ROLE: Member of village community, in this case, the innkeeper.

SITUATION: Informal social event - villagers meet at Inn, during the course of normal 'everyday' events.

HOW INTRODUCED: Innkeeper raises topic of state of causeway and spreads rumour of probable increase in toll charges.

CLASS ORGANISATION: Whole class in small groups, but within framework of a working day in the village, involving interaction between members of different groups.

DEVELOPMENT: Following the spread of the rumour, children are asked to consider how this will affect their lives, firstly in their smaller groups, and later by returning to a full, more formal village meeting to formulate their grievances and possible action.

CONTEXT: English Civil War – a Parliamentarian community.

PROBLEM: Warfare – a plot to rescue King Charles 1 will undo the gains made by Cromwell and lead to a resumption of hostilities.

SOURCE: This was a fictional event designed to focus attention on the issue of conflicting loyalties which was of genuine contemporary concern.

TEACHER ROLE: Local landowner in sympathy with Parliamentarian cause.

SITUATION: Formal social event – celebration of capture of King and later court case.

HOW INTRODUCED: Through 'arrival of a stranger' – second teacher in role as Royalist leader of plot to rescue King. In disguise she mingles with crowd to identify secret sympathisers.

CLASS ORGANISATION: Whole class involved in various celebratory activities.

DEVELOPMENT: Sympathisers are later brought to a secret meeting with second teacher and swear loyalty to the king. The plot is discovered and the teacher is brought to trial. Will her accomplices be discovered and will they keep their oath?

In each example, the drama work is planned to facilitate a particular aspect of historical understanding. The teacher in role and the children must respond to the issues within the constraints of the period under consideration and not only in the light of twentieth century experience, although obviously this cannot be left behind entirely. The drama will generate as many questions as it answers so that one of the results of the lesson should be a need to find out more. In this way, the drama work gives relevance to further research, as the evidence is used to serve a particular purpose, which the children can clearly recognise from their practical experiences in role.

PART 4: DRAMA TECHNIQUES

This section of the pamphlet aims to offer a few ideas to teachers wishing to plan their classroom drama work and complements Part 3. Individual techniques have been identified in bold type and organisational variants underlined for ease of reference.

Role play, in this sense, involves the child in adopting a point of view, and in speaking, behaving and responding to others in a way consistent with this particular stance. The language and behaviours developed by the child need to be spontaneous, not rehearsed or in any way previously specified, as can be the case with certain types of 'simulation' (see p.11). The spontaneity, however, needs to be rooted in the child's historical appreciation of the context of the project, which is why we insist that background research is such an important element of our methodology. Without preparation, the child's attempt to develop a role identity based on, for example, a twelfth century Cistercian monk, will inevitably owe more to fantasy than to any factual considerations. However, even though we are looking for a spontaneous response based on sound preparation, we need to prepare children for the demands of extended role play. In a sense, they need to learn to be spontaneous!

There are a number of excellent guides to classroom drama teaching techniques listed in our bibliography, to which teachers can refer for help and ideas in enabling children to become accustomed to working in role. For many teachers, the use of drama as an aid to the teaching of history will be an extension of work which is already regularly being carried out as part of their pupils' general experience, but for those teachers for whom the idea of using drama in this way is completely new we will briefly describe some techniques which will be found useful in preparatory classroom work.

With an inexperienced group, it is important to allay fears of 'having to stand up in front of the class', or 'making a fool of yourself' (we recognise that these are very real fears for some teachers too!). Early activities should concentrate on allowing each child to participate in a way in which he/she feels secure, emphasising that no-one will watch their work unless they wish others to do so and accepting contributions made by children at their face value. This latter point is especially important, for two reasons; it gives status to tentative suggestions made by less confident members of the group, and can also be a means of emphasising the serious nature of the work, by forcing pupils who make rather facetious points to justify or develop their argument. The teacher's seriousness is central to the development of commitment in the children. We have already said that the drama work will be fully developed only if the teacher also assumes a role identity as the work progresses. This too, must be taken seriously, by both teacher and pupils, so that thought needs to be given to the type of role which the teacher will adopt.

Since our work is based on the creation of individual identities within given social circumstances, we always begin by establishing a name and a place in society for each child. Ideally, this name and social status should be chosen by the children, or arrived at by negotiation, rather than imposed on them, although we have used the method of drawing identities 'from a hat' with younger children, in order to ensure that a range of identities and occupations were represented in the project (see p.23). It is most important that the children should feel actively involved and committed to the drama work from the beginning of the project, if we are to obtain successful learning outcomes.

Two very different techniques have been used effectively to generate this commitment in previous projects: **hot seating** an adult in role, and **collective map or model making.** The methods are not mutually exclusive, and could either be used to begin the drama work, or to reinforce role development in children in the early stages of preparation.

Hot seating involves literally placing someone on a chair and asking them questions about their life, actions, feelings and motives. The 'character' might be taken from literature, or from history; some previous preparation usually being required. This technique is used by Tim Wood in his book on <u>History Roleplays</u>, to which we have already referred.[29] We use this technique in a more open sense in our own drama teaching, to develop a role identity for the adult who will be working with the class during the project; to introduce children to the idea of the teacher in role, and to offer a practical example to the children of the kind of detail it is possible to develop within a personal identity.

Typically, the class will already have some background knowledge of the period under investigation in order to inform their questioning. The adult explains to the class that he/she will be working with them during the project and that he/she will have a particular name and job, just as the children will. The teacher asks the class if they would like to meet the person that he/she will be, during the project, and what questions they would like to ask that person.

At this point, teachers might wish to ask the class to prepare questions, individually or in pairs, to ensure a flow of dialogue, or they may wish to move straight into role. It is important to explain to the class that the teacher(s) will be working in role, alongside the children, before beginning the hot seating session, and it may be useful to establish a clear signal to indicate when the adult is 'in' role and when they are 'out'. These explanations help to minimise embarrassment on the part of the pupils and the teacher in dealing with what may be a new situation. Signals which can be used can be as simple as <u>"When I am sitting on this chair I will only answer as....</u>", or can involve objects or articles of clothing: <u>"When I am wearing this hat/ holding this staff....</u>".

Clothing and suitable objects can be a very useful aid to hot seating, both in terms of marking out a different teaching strategy, and also in involving the class in the process of role creation. In our own work, we almost invariably bring appropriate costume items into the classroom, and discuss the implications of these items with the class before putting them on (over our everyday clothing!).

Clearly some background preparation is essential on the part of the teacher in using this technique, as answers to questions need to be consistent with the identity being established. However, there is no need to have a prepared statement ready for every question. In most situations, having a general answer to a list of questions similar to that which we use to prepare the children for a History through Drama Day (see p.21) will be perfectly adequate. This is also an opportunity to emphasise by example the seriousness of the work, through the way in which the adult responds to the children's questions. Questions which are obviously either anachronistic, or facetious need to be dealt with face on at this early stage, either by being answered seriously, if possible, and thus defusing the situation, or by responding "I cannot answer that". Once out of role, teacher and class can discuss the reasons for a refusal to answer - was the question inappropiate, or was the character in some way unwilling or ignorant?

If children have already agreed (or been given) their own identities, the adult in the hot seat can ask his/her own questions in turn to help the children begin to identify with their own roles, but the hot seating technique can also be used as the first drama activity in a project, to stimulate interest and involvement, and to lead children naturally into the next stage, that of creating their own identities.

Collective map or model making may be a very useful aid to this process, but could also be the opening activity of a project. This could be based on contemporary sources (see p.22) but there are instances where one might wish to establish a 'community' without having any specific source material on which to base its location or arrangement, as in our Iron Age project. Through discussion and negotiation with the class, a large scale map or plan is drawn up, showing the principal features of the locality. To this map children add individual details - they identify their own street, house or area (the kitchens, or the herbarium for instance, if the location is based around a single building). Through identifying an area of concern, or a type of dwelling, the child also implies social status and occupation, and thus a commitment to the role identity has begun. Names, drawn from authentic sources are added, and thus every child can begin to recognise both his/her own place within the community, and also that of other members of the class.

Early drama work may well involve mainly group work (see p.25) and mimed activities, especially with younger pupils, although as we emphasise in Part 3, children will remain involved and committed to drama work for longer if there is a clear focus of interest (a problem or issue). Even at this stage, however, we want pupils to be aware of themselves as members of a community, and to be able to share their developing ideas. More confident or experienced pupils may well be happy to **re-enact** short scenes from their family or work-group discussions for the rest of the class. The use of the performance mode in this context would enable children to appreciate a range of differing points of view or responses to a problem before the community is brought together as a whole.

Less confident, or younger pupils may find the creation of a tableau or **still image** less daunting. Images can show 'significant moments', working activities, even emotional responses to situations; the technique is not solely of use to the inexperienced! Added to the image, the teacher can introduce the technique of **questioning in role**. A member of the group is touched, and asked an appropriate question, depending on the purpose of the image. The pupil must answer in role, and this questioning strategy is a very useful way of both encouraging children to speak in role and of deepening their sense of role identity. Questions can range from the simple "How long have you been working on this job? Is it very hard work?", to "What did you feel when you heard the news? How do you think your family will react?" Other members of the class can also be encouraged to ask questions of the group creating the image. Freed from the anxieties of having to 'act', individual children can share their ideas with the class, and with members of their own group for later development, by means of this useful technique.

Still image can also be used with the whole class, as well as with groups to slow down action if work seems to be losing direction: "Just hold that position for a moment, look carefully around you to see where other people are - think who you are, why you are here, what you are doing. When I touch you on the shoulder, just say a few words to describe what you are thinking about at this moment"; or to change focus: "Stop where you are for a moment. I am going to move the action on three hours, to a few minutes before the factory whistle blows for the end of the day. Think how you are feeling now; are you in the same place? Standing in the same way? If you have to move, move slowly and quietly to your new position. Everybody hold that picture - look carefully around you to see where other people are and how they look - now slowly bring the factory back to life."

So far, the **teacher's role** has not been considered, except possibly as that of the adult in the hot seat. We emphasise elsewhere (see p.22) that a successful History through Drama project involves all adults (teachers plus any others involved) creating a role in a similar way to the pupils. The teacher may decide on a role identity from the beginning (see Britford project, p.18) on the basis of organisational factors, or as preparation for hot-seating to be used early in the project. However, he/she could also deliberately wait for a possible role to emerge as preparatory work progresses, or decide on a role but delay introducing this to the children to allow for a greater variety of drama strategy.

The nature of the role adopted by the teacher affects both the structure of the subsequent work and the level of input available to the children. Whereas it can be useful to choose a role which offers opportunity for 'control' (such as the Reeve of the village), too high a status can effectively prevent the teacher from being able to enter into informal dialogue and/or prevent the pupils from being able to take on responsibility for the development of the drama themselves. Where the presence of a high status figure will be useful to a project, it will usually be preferable to involve another adult, such as an advisory teacher, if available. Failing this possibility, the more effective teacher role would be that of a 'middle-man', an intermediate role. This opens up the possibility of being able to represent the viewpoint of a fictional, higher status figure, while retaining sympathetic contact with the children as members of the larger group.

Another possible role to take is that of the <u>stranger</u> to the community: you might need help, and have arrived with a problem which only this community group can solve out of their own 'experience'; you might have arrived by chance and be looking for somewhere to settle; you might have news of significant events which have occurred elsewhere and which will affect the lives of people in this community. In any of the above variants, adopting the guise of a stranger opens the way for the children to take on more responsibility. They are the 'experts' in terms of the way their community operates, the skills of their job, their own community history. The teacher-as-stranger role enables **narrative** to be used both by pupils, in explaining to the stranger, and by the teacher in sharing his/her previous history or telling the important news. In this way, children deepen their own sense of community identity by developing a **collective memory** of previous events, such as how they dealt with poor harvests in the past, what they remember of previous battles with the invaders. Such 'memories' are based on background research, but have never been formally dramatised.

Quite often we use the **arrival of a stranger** to precipitate the events leading up to a final History through Drama Day, with the stranger bringing important news or an invitation to attend a celebration or community meeting. At the same time we always make sure that the 'stranger' has plenty of opportunity to talk informally with the children, in order for them to demonstrate their inside knowledge of their community. For any age of pupil, this status shift proves to be a very effective way of increasing children's sense of self esteem within the context of the drama.[30] Where no other adult presence is possible, the 'news' can of course be delivered by letter or 'invisible messenger': "<u>As I was making my way to market this morning, I was stopped by a man on horseback who seemed to be in a terrible hurry. He asked me to tell you all that......</u>".

These various techniques can be combined in a number of ways, along with small group work and whole class work, to focus on the types of problems and issues we have listed on p.24. We finish this section with two diagrammatic examples of lesson plans, showing how the different techniques and organisational patterns might be used:

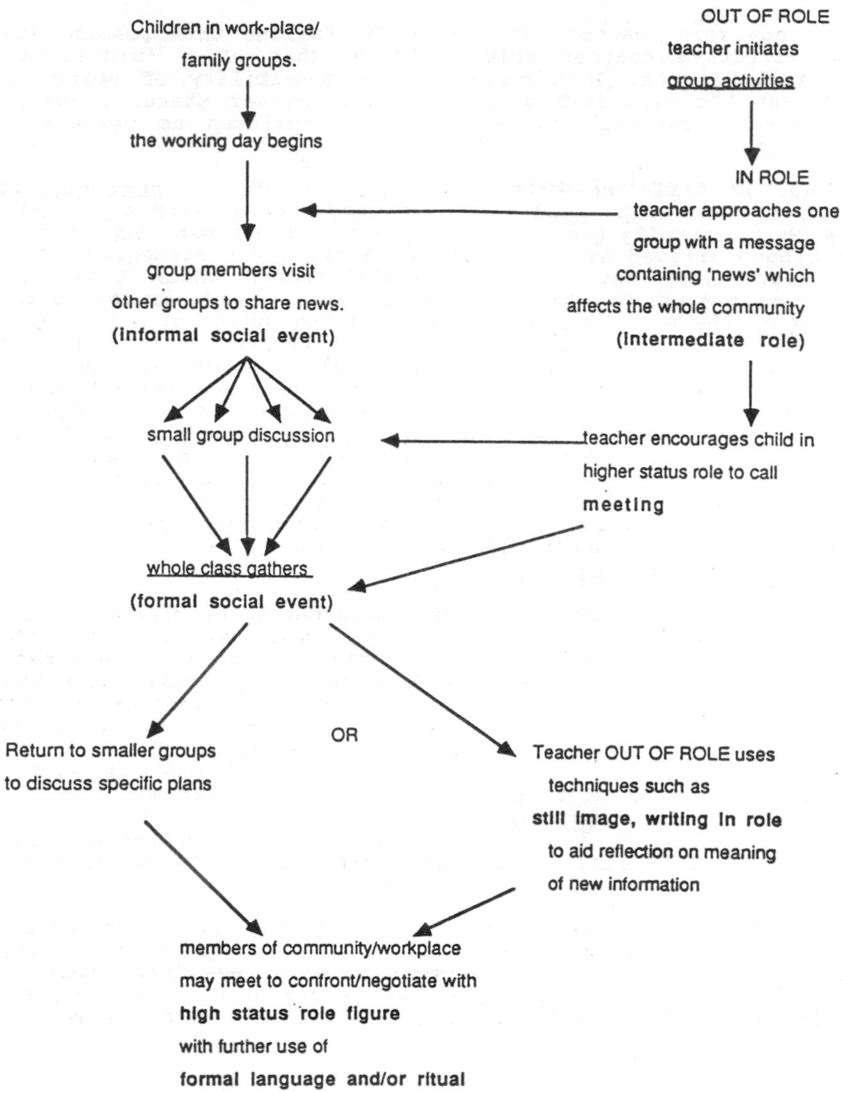

Children in work-place/
family groups.

OUT OF ROLE
teacher initiates
group activities

the working day begins

IN ROLE
teacher approaches one
group with a message
containing 'news' which
affects the whole community
(intermediate role)

group members visit
other groups to share news.
(informal social event)

small group discussion

teacher encourages child in
higher status role to call
meeting

whole class gathers
(formal social event)

Return to smaller groups
to discuss specific plans

OR

Teacher OUT OF ROLE uses
techniques such as
still image, writing in role
to aid reflection on meaning
of new information

members of community/workplace
may meet to confront/negotiate with
high status role figure
with further use of
formal language and/or ritual

(This could be one focus of a final History through Drama Day)

FIG. 2: SAMPLE LESSON OUTLINE1.

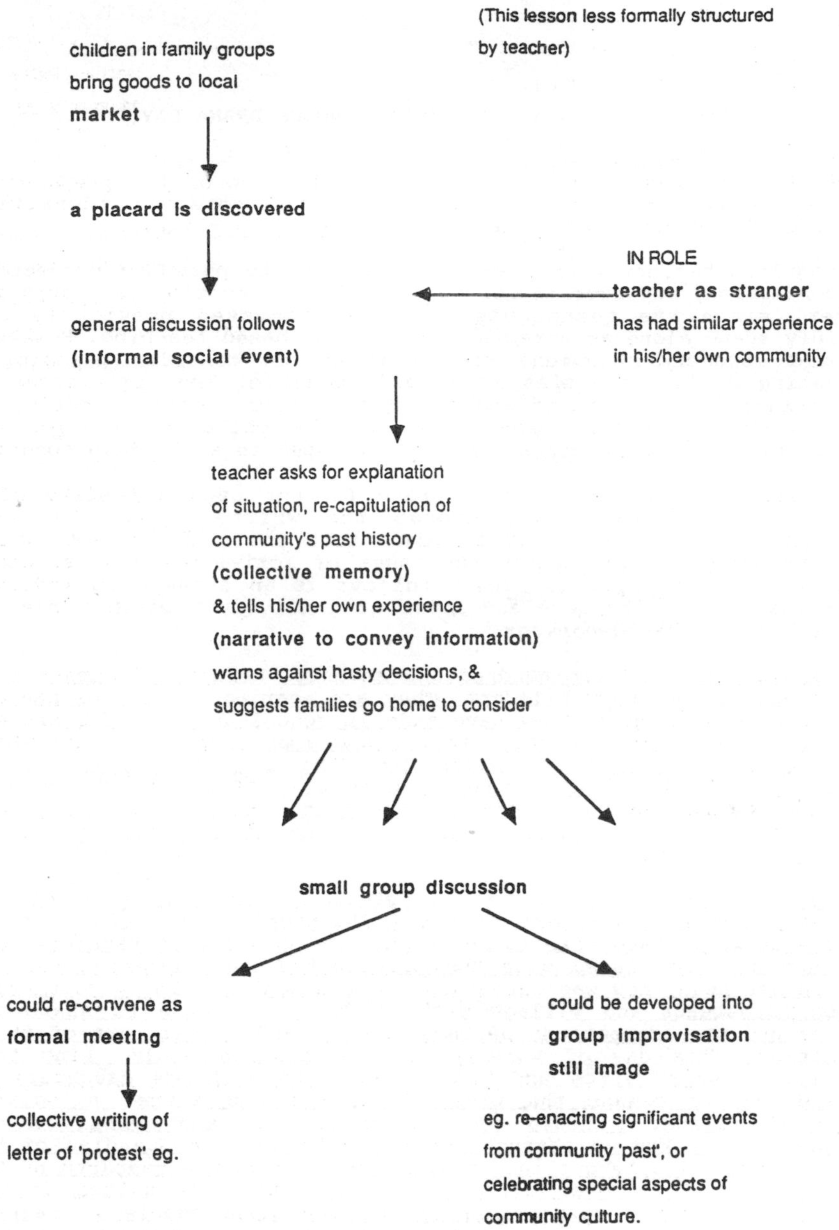

children in family groups
bring goods to local
market

(This lesson less formally structured
by teacher)

a placard is discovered

IN ROLE

teacher as stranger
has had similar experience
in his/her own community

general discussion follows
(informal social event)

teacher asks for explanation
of situation, re-capitulation of
community's past history
(collective memory)
& tells his/her own experience
(narrative to convey information)
warns against hasty decisions, &
suggests families go home to consider

small group discussion

could re-convene as
formal meeting

could be developed into
**group improvisation
still image**

collective writing of
letter of 'protest' eg.

eg. re-enacting significant events
from community 'past', or
celebrating special aspects of
community culture.

FIG. 3:   SAMPLE LESSON OUTLINE 2.

35

PART 5: PLANNING A HISTORY THROUGH DRAMA DAY

The 'History through Drama Day' is the culmination of the preparatory work, where teachers and children bring the personal identities developed in the classroom to inform an agreed storyline.

We recognise that not every teacher will wish to pursue a project to this conclusion, and have therefore written this section as a separate chapter, since the techniques we have discussed previously can certainly stand alone as aspects of classroom-based teaching. However, we would strongly recommend that teachers do consider planning a culminating day's activities if at all possible. The experiences of working in role, in costume and at an authentic location combine to form a particularly rich experience for the children in which the elements of classroom preparation are developed in a new relationship.

It is difficult to convey an accurate flavour of the quality of a History through Drama Day through the written word. We have participated in the making of a video about one such project, which more convincingly demonstrates the range of activities and responses of the children.[31] However, what follows is an attempt to indicate the intensity of atmosphere and level of involvement which a planned day's activities can generate:

The year is 1987, and two hundred and seventy children disembark from coaches outside Danebury hillfort. They are wearing simple costume and carrying artefacts which they have made in school as part of a project based on the Iron Age. As they start along a pre-arranged route which will lead them away from the modern buildings near the hillfort, and around the outside of the ramparts, they bring their knowledge from the classroom work to bear upon the re-enactment of a possible event from the past.....the year is 400BC......Tegwydd, a travelling healer and storyteller, speaks:

As I approached the last steep climb up to the entrance of the fortress I wondered how many of the tribespeople I had met in their settlements would have come to celebrate the Solstice at Danebury this year. How had Edda fared with the treatment I had suggested for the pains in her head, how was Caractacus' wound healing? In my journeying between farmsteads and village settlements I had come to share the troubles and pre-occupations of these people and I felt part of their communities. This day of worship and celebration would bring them together, to share gifts and trade goods, to exchange daughters in marriage and to cement the ties of kinship and mutual allegiance between the clans. I heard the sounds of drum and cymbal in the distance, and looked up through the trees to see the Guardian of the Grove standing clearly outlined against the sky on the ramparts of the fort. She and I followed different paths, but were united in our feelings of love and responsibility for the tribespeople we helped. Passing through the gates were a group of men and women whose standard of an oak tree identified them as a clan of the Brigantes. The

Guardian raised her hands in blessing over them and began the ritual greeting, but something was clearly wrong! Women were weeping and men shouting angrily on this day of all days... a day devoted to peace and prayers for prosperity. I hurried my steps towards the entrance so that I could hear what was happening:

"A band of robbers!" one man cried, "they took our food, which we had brought for the great feast."

"One of them tried to cut off my hair!" sobbed a young girl.

"They tried to take a hostage, but we broke free and ran".

The Guardian raised her hands to silence the outcries: "I will send a token to these marauders, calling them to answer to the gathering of the tribes for their misdeeds. Nothing must sully the peace of the celebration of the Solstice here at Danebury!"

For this group of children, this incident marked the first of several unexpected events which took place at Danebury Iron Age Hillfort in Hampshire. The main aim of the project had been to involve children in an investigation of a prehistoric period, and at the end of the final day, we felt that this had been quite successfully achieved. There were also other benefits, however, both for teachers and for children. The teachers expressed a strong sense of satisfaction with the way in which the project had involved working co-operatively with colleagues, both within individual schools, and also in conjunction with staff in other schools. For the children, the combination of the visual effect of the location and the intensity of a sustained drama, involving several 'unexpected' events, left them with a lasting memory of the total experience. Two of our contributors offer further examples of History through Drama Days at historic sites, both set in the sixteenth century, but offering contrasting experiences for the children involved (see pp.51-4, 61-3).

Starting points

For the teacher who wishes to pursue the planning of a final History through Drama event, it is important to stress that the storyline of the day must be decided upon at a very early stage. The roles that the children will need to take, and possibly many of the activities which will be part of the preparation will be determined by this overall structure. In effect, this means working backwards from the identified end. However, although planning for a form of predetermined outcome might appear to be restrictive, the framework still allows for a wide range of individual response from the children.

Most local environments will offer a starting point for a day's activities, with some investigation. It might be an historic site, a local legend or story, an authentic document, or an object around which a storyline can be built. Clearly the resources for finding this focus will vary considerably from area to area, but it is possible to make some generalisations about where to begin looking:

- Ordnance Survey maps, both recent and earlier editions, indicate the position of historic sites.

- Copies of the Victoria County History refer to historic events and sites in the locality.

- Local libraries, museums and record offices contain a wealth of material and specialist staff to give advice.

- Publications for the Tourist Information Service can be very helpful, particularly guide books, town trails etc.

- Local history societies can be founts of knowledge. Many produce their own publications.

- English Heritage and National Trust may have the care of sites in your area. Both bodies are becoming increasingly active in the educational field, and will sometimes allow sites to be used by schools (see Mike Corbishley's contribution on pp. 51-4).

- Living memory of people in the locality might provide suggestions of more recent events.

Clearly the children's experience will be greatly enhanced if it is possible to use an authentic historic location for the final day's role play, and this is an aspect of our approach that we ourselves aim for when we work with teachers. It may not even be necessary to look further than the immediate school environment as the grounds and buildings themselves can be used to good effect. There are still a number of original school buildings in use dating from the Victorian period onwards and these can provide the focus for a History through Drama Day based on how children were taught in the past. In some schools contemporary records exist, such as the log books, admission registers, photographs and pupil reports, and these can form the historical evidence on which the project can draw.

When, for reasons of finance or feasibility, the use of an authentic location is not viable there are still alternatives which can prove successful. For example, an imaginative school recently involved in a project on the Romans, converted their modern classrooms into a Romano-British villa, complete with hypocaust and steam room![32] In this instance, the range of activities which took place were much greater than would have been the case at the site of a real villa, where usually only the foundations of buildings and rooms remain.

If there is no suitable site in the vicinity, it may also be possible to substitute any available open space as the basic location. We have found that removing children from the immediate school environment, even if not to an actual historic site, has considerable benefits for the drama. A city centre school, presently planning a project on Saxons and Normans, is using a local 'green space' area as the prospective site of a motte and bailey castle. The day's activities will centre on the arrival of the Norman overlord, the planning and preparation for building his castle on the site, and the reaction of the Saxon inhabitants.

In conclusion, there are certain basic criteria which must be considered when deciding where to work:

1. There must be privacy, so that the activities are not interrupted by onlookers.

2. The trappings of present day life should be excluded as far as possible.

3. The opportunity for children to reach the site on foot, rather than be dropped 'at the door' by coach, is not essential, but highly recommended.

4. The safety aspect must be fully investigated.

However, this does not preclude the possibility of devising your own storyline. For example, the events planned by Roger Day surrounding the trial and attempted execution of a notorious highwayman were suggested by the proximity of an eighteenth century house and grounds.[33] No historical evidence for this character existed, but the fiction provided the focus around which research into the period could be based. This approach can have several advantages, of course, in that the programme of events can be structured to provide specific drama experiences for the children, as well as encouraging historical understanding.

Further planning

Having decided upon your basic storyline, you also need to consider in the early stages of planning the other activities which will take place on the final day. These decisions are best made at the beginning of a project, since much of the subsequent classroom work can be geared towards preparation for these events. Whatever your period, whatever your location, we suggest there are certain general activities which could be incorporated:

THE WALK. As part of the process of helping children leave the present day behind and enter into role more fully, a walk leading to the chosen site is most effective. The schools taking part in the Danebury project arranged for the coaches to drop them some distance from the hillfort. The children approached the site by walking along a trackway and circling the ramparts. This provided an opportunity for them to absorb their Iron Age identities - as well as allowing for the surprise attack by a band of ruthless marauders. If possible, we suggest a walk of up to one mile so that the children arrive on site already in role.

THE FAIR. Whether you are working with other schools, other classes or on your own, the children need to be immediately involved in the period as soon as they arrive on site. A suggested starting point is a market or fair where goods made in the classroom can be 'bought' or exchanged. The use of an appropriate coinage system can add significantly to the value of this exercise. Period games and sports could be included at this point, or might be used later on in the day.

WORKSHOP ACTIVITIES. In many cases teachers may find it useful to incorporate a variety of practical craft-based activities on site. These provide the opportunity for children to have hands-on experience of the technologies appropriate to the period under study. Workshops could include spinning and weaving, pottery manufacture, brick making, calligraphy, cookery, herbalism, farming, or any other contemporary activities applicable to the location. At a Day based at Netley Abbey, for example, workshops included stone carving and building, since the event centred around the foundation of the Abbey itself. This element has proved very popular in a wide range of contexts, both because it focusses the children's attention on a single activity and so can be particularly suitable for younger children, and also because it allows for a greater degree of organisational control on the teachers' part. The quality of this experience will, however, be limited, unless workshop leaders have developed their own role identities. Where parents or other outside agencies provide support for workshops, they also need to be involved in preparatory work.

THE MID-DAY MEAL. This can be organised in such a way that it becomes both historically accurate (within the limitations of modern dietary requirements!) and part of the dramatic experience. It would be quite inappropriate for Saxon villagers or Iron Age tribespeople suddenly to produce a can of coca-cola and a packet of crisps. We therefore try to ensure that food items and their containers are given as much consideration as costume and trade goods. This offers an added dimension to classroom research, through investigating the type of food available in different periods, together with methods of cooking, preserving, serving and eating.[34] Suitable containers can also be prepared, for instance plastic drinking bottles can be covered with string or fabric, and food carried to the site in baskets or tied cloths. These measures help to ensure that the continuity of the day is maintained and that the meal remains in keeping with the character of the day.

THE ENTERTAINMENT. Music, songs and storytelling might offer a period for quieter participation and enjoyment immediately after the meal. There is also likely to be a place for dancing, theatrical entertainments such as mummers plays or melodramas, puppet shows, juggling and similar events. These might be incorporated into the morning's fair, or offered as special entertainments to a visiting dignitary.

ISSUES. During the preparatory work in school, children may well have explored certain issues (see Part 3). The final Day may offer the opportunity for resolving disputes which have been previously developed. Public courts or investigations may become part of the day's programme in which complaints are heard and justice is dispensed. Alternatively, community concerns which have been explored during the classroom drama can now be brought to a final resolution, perhaps through the decisions of a large meeting.

THE CONCLUSION. As many of the Day's activities are likely to have involved small group work, it is always a valuable experience to bring all the participants together in a satisfying collective event. This might well be some form of ceremonial - a religious service/dedication for example, or a formal leave-taking of the visiting dignitary - or could be the administering of punishments for those found guilty by the court.

Saxons and Normans at Old Sarum - the Britford Project

To show how all these varying factors can be used in practice, an account of one particular project has been used. This was taught in a village school in the Salisbury area, with four other small schools also involved in similar preparations leading up to a final day at Old Sarum. The topic was based on the Saxons and Normans, and was chosen for three reasons:

There was a suitable **SITE** within travelling distance of the schools involved - the motte and bailey castle at Old Sarum.

There was an **ACTUAL EVENT** to base the Day's events upon, since William the Conqueror had visited Old Sarum in 1087.

All the schools involved were in villages listed in the Domesday survey, so there was **PRIMARY SOURCE** material locally available. The school environs were used to consider how the area had changed since the eleventh century; in the case of the particular school whose work we describe, fieldwork in Britford village and its Saxon church proved particularly valuable. Artefacts were examined in Salisbury Museum and local sites visited.

SECONDARY RESOURCES used included programmes in the BBC T.V. series Zig-Zag on the theme of Saxons and Normans, plus a full range of books, slides, illustrations etc.

The **STORYLINE** for the final day involved the villagers travelling to Old Sarum to pay allegiance to William the Conqueror. This was taken as an opportunity to hold a fair, and to have inter-village games and sports.

The **ISSUES** that were explored during the preparatory work were identified as:

1. Daily life in the eleventh century from the viewpoints of a) Saxon villagers, b) Norman settlers.

2. The racial conflicts resulting from the act of conquest and the imposition of a new culture upon a conquered people.

3. The concept of a feudal society.

4. How the local area has changed since this time.

PERSONAL HISTORIES were begun by the children drawing names from a box. The Domesday extract for Britford gave details of numbers of freemen, villeins, cottars and slaves in the village. Actual names were taken from contemporary literature, and status derived from the Domesday extract. The children's roles were not voluntarily chosen, but this reflected the inflexibility of a feudal system. The teacher's role was selected to permit her to act as an authority figure, but not to be too remote, and she became the Reeve of the village. From this point onwards, the register was called using Saxon names.

Work started with developing a concept of feudal society. A large ladder was drawn up in the classroom, and the children placed a figure of themselves on the appropriate rung; ie. slaves at the very bottom, freemen higher up, Norman rulers higher still and finally the King at the top. This formed the basis of how characters would relate to one another in the village - who would have authority in decision making and the amount of possessions individuals would own.

Fieldwork in Britford village itself established certain fixed points for the Saxon village, eg. the position of the church and the course of the river. Subsequent drama work built on this to create a map of the village in 1087. Children decided on the sites of their homes, fields and routes in and out of the village. In the early stages of the project we therefore have a sense of geographical **LOCATION** and a **COMMUNITY** with a **SOCIAL HIERARCHY** established.

To develop **DRAMA** work, much use was made of the school grounds. On the final Day the children would be out of doors in unfamiliar circumstances and it was important not to confine the drama to the classroom or school hall. The children needed to experience working in role in larger, open-air spaces. A 'village' was created in the school grounds, using skipping ropes for streets, hoops for the church and carpet tiles to mark the position of houses. These essentially simple devices established boundaries, but were easy to take out and put away quickly whenever necessary. Much of the drama took place in these surroundings and small groups of children were sometimes sent to work here apart from the rest of the class.

Work progressed to develop a sense of **COMMUNITY**. The drama focussed on decision making as it would affect a rural society, for instance, after a poor harvest, should corn be saved for seed, with possible starvation of some villagers, or eaten? Reactions to the Norman invasion were explored through story telling which recounted eye witness versions of the Battle of Hastings, and of King Harold's behaviour and experiences. All this was supported by **CLASSROOM RESEARCH** into the period, sometimes as the starting point of a drama and sometimes developing out of it as the need to find out more arose.

COSTUME making went on in the classroom. All the children made their own simple tunics from old sheets, dyed with natural dyes. It was important that the children had plenty of experience of wearing their costumes before the final day, and the class made their own decision that costumes could be worn when work on the topic was being carried out, and that when in costume, children would answer only to their Saxon names!

42

Through the preparatory work in the classroom many opportunities for **CROSS-CURRICULAR** work arose. For example, in the practical mathematics involved in land allocation and grain yields, and through scientific experiments into the dyeing process, children were working with a specific end in view. This gave the work a coherence and purpose which can be lacking in some classroom activities.

In the week preceding the visit to Old Sarum, the children were given the opportunity to spend an extended period in role. The arrival of two **STRANGERS** helped to focus the drama and provide a foretaste of the main event. Sir Raoul de Ville and his companion, Sir Guillaume de Bois (the County Drama and INSET Advisers respectively) had come to question villagers about their work and payment of taxes. Sir Raoul, who had recently arrived from Normandy, spoke very little English. This reinforced the children's awareness of the position of a conquered people. As a result of this language problem one of the village women was accused of attempting to steal Sir Raoul's horse. After much confusion and misunderstanding the villagers begged to have their case tried before the King.

As the children set out for the final **HISTORY THROUGH DRAMA DAY** at Old Sarum, they took with them items of craft work they had made in class to trade with other villagers, and food for the mid-day meal which was appropriate to the period; bread, cheese, apples, eggs and apple juice. In addition, a special gift had been made for presentation to the King. The drama began with a **WALK**. Saxons from surrounding villages approached the castle using a number of different footpaths away from the car park and toilets. Ensuring that the coaches dropped the children some distance from the site meant that in the process of about a mile's walk, traffic, modern houses and passers-by were all left behind. The experience of seeing different groups arriving from various directions in costume and with banners waving added a further important dimension to the beginning of the day.

A **FAIR** provided the opportunity to meet children from other schools whilst **TRADING** the items brought from the preparatory work. A **SERVICE** was held in the ruined cathedral, after which the King arrived (a teacher from a local secondary school) and representatives from each village pledged their loyalty to him.

This **CEREMONY** was followed by an open-air **FEAST** during which each village provided **ENTERTAINMENT** for the King and other villagers. The highlight of this occasion was an exhibition of hawk flying by two boys. Britford village caused some offence by singing a song about King Harold, but was later pardoned! **DISPUTES** were heard by the King, whose rulings were law, and inter-village **GAMES AND SPORTS** completed the day's activities.

Administrative details

So far we have considered the planning of storyline, activities and choice of site which will directly influence the earlier classroom work in terms of both drama and historical research. Alongside these decisions, administrative details must also be considered to ensure the successful outcome of a History through Drama Day. In the first instance teachers need to decide whether they wish to work alone, or join with other colleagues in a co-operative effort. The latter choice could involve a group of teachers in the same school, a number of schools working jointly, or a combination of both. The work we have developed has always drawn on co-operation between teachers as we believe this has many distinct advantages. The workload involved in planning and preparation can be shared, as can organisational responsibilities. Where different schools choose to work together, early contact between pupils can be developed through a variety of forms, such as letter writing, exchange of portraits, and visits. Children can also greatly benefit from the opportunity to work within a larger group on the final day, which might include a range of different ages.

The following is a breakdown of the planning involved in the preparation for a project with a History through Drama Day as its focus. Many aspects are self-explanatory, but we have enlarged on some details where necessary, and these are indicated by asterisks. The details are written on the basis of one teacher working independently, but additional factors which need to be taken into account in a co-operative project are included in italics.

First stage*:

1. Obtain agreement of headteacher(s) <u>and other staff</u>/schools and set up series of <u>regular meetings</u>.

2. Identify starting point and suitable location for final day.

3. Select date for final day.

4. Obtain permission for use of site, and investigate what insurance cover is necessary for activities to take place there.*

5. Make preliminary visit to site.

6. Ascertain facilities on site.**

7. Contact other support agencies, eg. museums service, local advisory teachers, archive staff, teacher training institutions, etc.

8. <u>Divide workload</u> and begin to collect resources.

*Planning needs to take place AT LEAST one full term before the proposed date of the final day. This is particularly important where the use of an authentic historical site is being considered, as a lengthy period of notice is usually required by those agencies responsible for the care and management of such locations. It is often a condition of use that specific insurance cover must be negotiated as indemnity against damage to the site.

** Facilities might include the presence of a tap on site, so that water would not need to be carried, and toilet arrangements. Many locations will not be provided with sanitary facilities and alternatives may need to be considered. We have found that this has never proved to be the problem which is often anticipated. Provided that children use the lavatory before leaving school, there is too much going on for most of them to give it a further thought.

Second stage:

1. Decide on a storyline for the final day.

2. Obtain parental permission and invite parental involvement.*

3. Identify roles for pupils and adults.

4. Determine range of activities to take place on final day.

5. <u>Arrange to develop initial contacts between pupils in different classes/schools</u>.**

* One of the major difficulties which we have encountered is the presence of unprepared adults on the final day. Continued adult commitment to working in role is a necessary condition for sustaining the drama for the children. Where adults are seen not to be taking the situation seriously, this communicates itself to the children and makes their continued involvement more difficult. We recognise that History through Drama Days outside the school grounds would be an impossibility without the involvement of parents or other helpers in order to reach the required safe level of supervision. It is therefore most important to involve other adults in the preparatory work, and to pay as much attention to the roles which they will take as to the roles of the children and teachers. We realise that in a large project this will be a major undertaking for teachers and we recognise the challenge we have presented in this statement. Nevertheless, we must emphasise the qualitative difference which can be made to the day when all adults are fully aware of the purpose and nature of the experience.

**This might take the form of organising children into shared family groups across the different schools. Families could then exchange letters, tokens, or photographs/pictures of themselves in role.

Third stage:

1. Commence preparatory work in schools.*

2. Obtain LEA permission/insurance for children to be out of school.

3. Arrange transport to site.

4. Formulate contingency plans for wet weather.**

5. Make preliminary walk to check time and distance along chosen route.

6. Begin planning for costumes.

* In our experience this occupies about half a term, although some teachers may prefer to work less intensively for a longer period.

** Although we try to arrange History through Drama Days at the times of the year when dry weather might be expected, we always make some contingency arrangements in the event of a downpour. During drizzle or light rain the day's activities can proceed with very little loss of enjoyment, as the investment of all concerned in a successful outcome is already very high. However, despite the fact that a school hall is a poor substitute for an Iron Age hillfort, and will of necessity curtail much of the day's programme, it may be the only viable alternative to complete cancellation. It may be encouraging to add that, as yet, we have never had to use our own contingency measures.

Two weeks before final day:

1. Finalise arrangements for food on the Day, either via letter to parents with suggestions for packed lunch or by purchasing/preparing suitable items in school.

2. Agree on final timetable for Day's events.

3. Contact local publicity sources.*

4. Arrange transportation of any large/heavy items needed for various activities.

*Many schools may wish to notify local press, radio and/or television. It is useful to have a press statement already prepared to avoid interruption to the proceedings and ensure accuracy of reporting! It is also worthwhile contacting these agencies personally to emphasise the nature of the event and to request sympathetic coverage - for instance by not asking children to pose for photographs. Reporters approached in this way have even been known to appear in costume.

Final week:

1. Last minute check of costume, trade items, games and sports paraphernalia, food arrangements, transport, wet weather plans, individual adults' responsibilities.

2. Extended in-role experience in costume and preferably out-of-doors.*

3. Don't panic!!!

*We have already pointed out that children should be encouraged to become used to wearing their costumes well before the final day in order to minimise any sense of 'dressing up'. One such occasion can be used as the opportunity for an extended in-role experience immediately prior to the final Day. During this activity, children can meet with other adults involved in the event, and possibly become aware of some new issue(s), the outcome(s) of which will be resolved on the Day.

Iron Age Solstice celebration at Danebury Hillfort

As an example of the inter-relationship between storyline and
necessary preparatory activities, two handouts from planning meetings
for the above project are given. Three schools were involved, and some
270 children took part in the solstice celebrations, making the need
for thorough planning vital. Approximate times are included for the
final Day, although clearly these had to be flexible. The following
related activities represent a small sample of the classroom-based
research and role-play which took place.

DANEBURY - STORYLINE

10.00 am.   Coaches drop tribes some distance from hillfort. Tribes
walk towards Danebury from different directions.

Marauders attack as many as possible.

11.00 am.   Tribes aim for gateway approach into Danebury. Guardian
of the Grove (JW) and others line entrance, salutes and
greetings exchanged.

Tribes proceed to inner meeting place and are met.

Tribes erect totems and claim an area which will be
their 'territory' for the day and used as a gathering
point.

Tribes called together and welcomed by Guardian. Tribal
messengers brought out. Complaints called for.

Scouts sent out to locate marauders carrying peace
token.

Marauders enter hillfort, offer explanations and are
accepted into the celebrations.

Games, sports, initiations, inter-tribal trade.

12.00 am.   Celebratory feast.

1.00 pm.   Ardan, master story-teller (Roger Day) tells a story to
all, then begins the story-telling competition.

Story-tellers are judged and the winner applauded.

2.00 pm.   Finally, all circle the ramparts in the great dance,
and salute the sun.

In order for this storyline to work on the Day, each school needed
to provide/do the following things:

- Make a tribal totem.

- Provide the resources for a contemporary game or sport and be prepared to organise it at Danebury.

- Prepare items for trade exchange and gift exchange.

- Nominate a number of tribal messengers (one per class).

- Nominate leading tribal storytellers (no more than two per class).

- Nominate anyone a) about to enter manhood (male), b) who wishes to enter the service of the Grove (female).

- Prepare items of food/drink which are as authentic as possible with appropriate containers.

- Prepare costume items for all adults and children.

- Plan a walk to the hillfort from the coach park.

Mike Corbishley's account provides a further example of the links between site, storyline and preparation (see pp.51-4).

It is clear from this section of the pamphlet that working towards a History through Drama Day involves a great deal of professional commitment from teachers in terms of the necessary preparation and organisation. We are, however, confident that the rewards are proportionately great. Children who have taken part in such projects have responded with levels of motivation and interest that purely classroom-based activities can rarely generate. For many of them the final Day becomes an experience to remember, and one that they can recall with great pleasure even years later. The lasting impression that History through Drama creates in children's minds is that learning about the past is both exciting and enjoyable, and something in which they can be actively and practically involved. A teaching strategy which generates this level of response has a vital contribution to make to the learning process. We conclude with the hope that this pamphlet will encourage more teachers to draw upon the ideas and suggestions we make here.

REFERENCES

1. Fines, J., and Verrier, R., (1974), The Drama of History, New University Education.

2. See bibliography for details.

3. This aspect is explored further by Little, V., (Aut. 1983), 'History through Drama with top juniors', T. Hist., Vol. 11, No. 2, pp.16-7.

4. DES, (1985), History in the Primary and Secondary Years: An HMI View, HMSO.

5. For a general publication reflecting this approach, see Greater Manchester Primary Contact, Special Issue No. 6, (1986), History and the Primary School.

6. Southern Regional Examination Board, (1986), Empathy in History: From Definition to Assessment.

7. For a philosophical discussion of empathy see Shemilt, D., (1984), 'Beauty and the philosopher: empathy in history and classroom', IN Dickenson, A.K., Lee, P.J., and Rogers, P.J., (eds.), Learning History, Heinemann.

8. DES, (1985), op.cit., p.3.

9. Blyth, A., et al, (1976), Place, Time and Society 8-13, Schools Council, p.113.

10. The Independent, 10 March 1988.

11. Jenkins, K., and Brickley, P., (Jul. 1988), 'A Level history: on historical facts and other problems', T. Hist., No. 52, p.23.

12. DES, (1988), History from 5 to 16: Curriculum Matters 11, an HMI series, HMSO.

13. For a recent discussion on the empathy issue, see articles in T. Hist., (Ap. 1989), No. 55.

14. Barker, B., and Boden, R., (1973), 'Railway mania', History Games, Longman.

15. Wood, T., (1982), Playback: History Roleplays, Arnold, Chapter 5, 'Westford Workhouse', pp.39-42.

16. MARY ROSE, (1983), Ginn, Aylesbury.

17. SAQQARA, (1983), Expedition to Saqqara, Ginn, Aylesbury.

18. Coate, L., Ellis, M., Simkin, J., (1984), <u>Attack on the Somme: Computer Assisted Learning</u>, Trellis Pubs., Brighton.

19. Redfearn, N., (Summer 1982), 'Saxon Action', <u>London Drama</u>, Vol. 6, No. 6, pp.11-14.

20. Rogers, P.J., (Oct. 1977), 'Play, enactive representation and learning', <u>T. Hist.</u>, No. 19, pp.18-21.

21. Birt, D., and Nichol, J., (1975), <u>Games and Simulations in History</u>, p.6.

22. Culpin, C.B., (June 1984), 'Language, learning and thinking skills in history', <u>T. Hist.</u>, No. 39, p.27.

23. <u>Ibid.</u>, p.25.

24. ILEA, (1984), <u>The Waste-ground</u>, Learning Resources Branch.

25. O'Neill, C., and Lambert, A., (1982), <u>Drama Structures</u>, Hutchinson, pp.83-105.

26. Some of the projects in which we have been involved (Saxons and Normans at Britford, Tudor Court Leet, Iron Age sostice at Danebury) are published elsewhere. See bibliography for full references.

27. Sichel, M., <u>Costume Reference</u>, Batsford, is a useful series providing details of historical costume.

28. Patterns for similar simple costumes can be found in Fairclough, J., and Redsell, P., (1985), <u>Living History - reconstructing the past with children</u>, Historic Buildings and Monuments Commission, pp.34-5.

29. Wood, (1982), <u>op. cit.</u>

30. See references to the 'mantle of the expert' within the work of drama practitioners such as Dorothy Heathcote, for example, Wagner, B.J., (1979), <u>Dorothy Heathcote: Drama as a Learning Medium</u>, Hutchinson.

31. The Tudor Court Leet - see bibliography.

32. Personal communication, Roger Day.

33. This particular event is fully described in Day, R., 'History through Drama: it's more than cowboys and indians, IN D'Arcy, P., et al, <u>What's Going On</u>? Boynton Cook.

34. For examples of cooking methods plus contemporary recipes see the <u>Food and Cooking</u> series published by English Heritage.

THE PAST REPLAYED

English Heritage and living history projects for schools

Mike Corbishley, Head of Education, English Heritage.

*'History comes to life when you become a
person from a different age in a genuine setting.'*

... so says the commentator in one of our films for teachers.
We believe it, too, but we also know that it is not easy.

How do we set about it?

English Heritage Education Service has organised living history
projects all over the country for a number of years. Our initial
'training' came from John Fairclough and Patrick Redsell's work at one
of our monuments, Orford Castle. Since then we have joined with a
number of LEAs and museum education services to provide large scale
projects at our monuments. Our Projects have stretched from third
century AD North Leigh Roman Villa to Avebury Stone Circle in the
eighteenth century, from Tudor Minster Lovell Hall to Osbourne House
in the late nineteenth century. Sometimes we respond to requests from
schools or individual teachers, sometimes our Regional Education
Officers decide to set up a project.

Choosing the site

The choice of site is very important. All our sites are authentic, of
course but not all are suitable for large-scale events. Above all it
must be possible for all participants (children, teachers, group
leaders, actors and actresses) to feel that they really are 'in a
different age'. While it may not be possible to stop American planes
from entering the twelfth century air-space of Orford Castle, the
organisers must create a physical space which excludes, as far as
possible, the 20th century. All the practical aspects must be looked
into at this stage - what happens when it rains, how do they get to
the loos, how can we keep the general public away, where will the
first aid tent be and can we convince the first-aider to attend in
historic costume? Things can go wrong, of course. On a project I ran
at Tilbury Fort, in Essex, as the children were being lined up (in the
mid eighteenth century) and barked at by a fierce sergeant, a British
Telecom van drove right across the parade ground!

Choosing the storyline

There must be a credible reason for a large number of children to be
gathered at a site. The line taken by the Orford Castle project has
been re-used many times: the castle may be attacked at any moment and,
since the defences are unfinished, apprentices have been brought in
from the surrounding villages and towns to help. An encampment is set
up where a number of different activities can take place.

51

In this storyline the occupiers (Normans, for example) also want to instruct those whose country they have occupied (Saxons) in the 'new ways'. This conveniently allows for a whole variety of activities and, therefore, learning opportunities. Other storylines may emerge from the history of the site. Some dramatic elements are usually inserted into the day, perhaps as sub-plots.

Detailed planning

The project at Kirby Hall in Northamptonshire will serve as an example of the various stages of a living history project.

Kirby Hall - a role-play project for children with special educational needs

This project stemmed from a request to English Heritage. Malcolm Tyler, the County Music Inspector, and Judith Horner, an Advisory Teacher for Music, wanted to hold a concert at Kirby Hall, to be given by various special needs schools. The idea for a costumed role-play event just grew from discussions! In the end we decided to involve 120 children from eight schools in a full-day's event.

The practical arrangements and costs were shared between English Heritage and Northamptonshire LEA. For example, English Heritage provided all the material for the children's costumes and arranged some special leaders for the day; Northamptonshire arranged teachers' courses and provided actors, from Theatre-in-Education at the Theatre Royal, Northampton.

Discussions about the project began in the summer term of 1986 and the project started in September. Regular teachers' meetings were held and special courses were arranged so that teachers could find out about primary sources and resources for the period. A storyline was devised and a programme agreed with all the teachers and organisers involved. It was:

*   Each school would make costumes for the boys and girls taking part on the day. Material patterns and background information were provided but the schools had to decide whether the children would be able to make their own costumes. Teachers and group leaders made their own costumes.

*   Each school would provide one sixteenth century dish for lunch on the day. English Heritage would supplement the food and provide bowls and platters.

*   Teachers' courses would cover food and cooking, dancing, making costumes, music of the period and historical background.

*   Each 'work group' on the day would have two leaders, all teachers or ex-teachers.

*   The date chosen was 1590 and the storyline was that the owners of Kirby Hall, Sir Christopher and Lady Hatton, had invited children 'from the locality' to come and see their fine house (still partly

under construction to account for the ruinous state of some of it!).
The owners had arranged entertainment for the children when they
arrived. The children then went into a number of 'work-groups' to
learn something of life at that time in a grand house - they learnt to
write using quill pens, they played indoor games and danced, they
studied make-up, hygiene and herbs, they tried their hand at miniature
painting and tried on costumes of lords and ladies. Each child went to
two work-groups before lunch.

*   After lunch in the grand hall it was the children's turn to
entertain their hosts - they danced and sang, they recited verses,
they tumbled, juggled and bowled hoops, they presented a masque and
displayed models, paintings and purses they had made at school or
during the morning.

The project day (June 17th) seemed a long way off during the courses
and meetings in the autumn term but by the spring classrooms were
beginning to fill with work related to the project and the period.
Getting out of the buses on the day itself some of the children felt
'embarrassed with these clothes on' or just 'nervous'. Passing through
the great doorway into the inner courtyard or Kirby Hall they were
greeted by Sir Christopher and Lady Hatton. It was 1590 - just as we
had promised them. The rooks flew noisily overhead and music floated
out from the hall. There were no telephones ringing and they had
already forgotten the bus ride. I'm not sure whether all the adults
were able to slip so easily into role! The day passed without mishap
- although shoppers in a nearby Tesco were surprised by a group leader
buying an essential but forgotten item in full dress at eleven o'clock
in the morning!

Each school began its follow-up work the next day and all contributed
to an exhibition of work and photographs in Northampton Teachers'
Centre in the autumn term. A travelling display for teachers was also
prepared. Was it all worth it? I think all the participating schools
would agree that the project focussed the children's minds, and their
own, on one period and also allowed them to develop and practice
skills. All sorts of work was carried out in the main subject areas
such as art and craft work, creative writing, history and maths. In
this and other areas all the children achieved something tangible
which others could see. An important aspect was that 'others' included
other staff, mums and dads, school governors and LEA office staff.

The Kirby Hall project is the subject of a video made especially to
help teachers plan special projects like this and below is a list of
other relevant publications and videos from English Heritage.

Publications

Fairclough, J., and Redsell, P., (1985), '<u>Living History-reconstructing the past with children</u>', Historic Buildings and Monuments Commission.

Videos

<u>Living History</u>, (1986), tape-slide programme converted to video on various living history projects including some smaller-scale ones teachers might try in schools. <u>The Past Replayed</u>, (1988), Kirby Hall project.

Both these videos are available on free loan, or may be purchased at £9.95. The cost of videos and publications includes p & p. In addition the following video is available on free loan only.

<u>The Kenilworth Project</u>, (1988), made by Coventry Teachers' Centre about a large-scale project organised jointly by Coventry LEA and English Heritage. A visit to the castle by Queen Elizabeth I.

Videos available from: English Heritage, PO Box 43, Ruislip, Middlesex HA4 OXW.

ENCLOSURE THROUGH DRAMA

Alan Dennis, Head of History, Purbrook Secondary School, Hampshire.
Ray Verrier, currently working on the ETHOS Project.

'The North Field has been sold for 105 guineas, someone said.
People think that because we're simple we can be conned. People
can't decide whether it's the east field being sold or north
field. Lots of rumours are going round. We think that Squire
Katner is a Londoner and he's going to buy north field and chuck
us off'.

Diary of Claire Morgan - Weaver, Blockney villager 1740.

Claire is in fact a 12 year old pupil who had been taking a villager's
role in a piece of drama designed to explore some of the problems
brought about through eighteenth century enclosures. At the end of
each session one of the pupils was asked to write a diary entry to
show how the writer felt about the events that had taken place in the
imaginary village of Blockney.

The Enclosure drama project took place over six weekly 40 minute
lessons and was team-taught by Alan Dennis and Ray Verrier. Two mixed
ability classes of 12 year old pupils were separately involved, the
development of the work taking a similar form with each class. The
example used here charts the development of the project with one of
the classes.

Context of the project

The history module Alan was studying with both classes was based on
the impact of new technology on society in Britain between 1740 and
1900. Historical content was drawn from the agricultural, transport
and industrial revolutions. Alan had four main aims:

1. To develop the pupils' understanding of human activity in
   the past.

2. To develop understanding of the nature of evidence and the
   associated study skills.

3. To help pupils appreciate the social and cultural values of
   the time.

4. To introduce pupils to the concept of cause and consequence.

At a planning meeting before the start of the project Alan and Ray
agreed to use six lessons for empathy work that was designed to help
pupils' understanding of the third aim - appreciation of the social
and cultural values of the time. Drama was to be used as a means
towards empathetic understanding. The particular topic in this module
to be studied was eighteenth century enclosure.

Resources used

The basic printed text used by both classes was Jon Nicol's <u>Developing Britain 1740 to 1900</u>. Other types of resource were developed by Ray and Alan which included the creation of a page from a vestry rate book from the village of Blockney, a large blackboard-sized map of the village that could be added to by the pupils, an enclosure award map which was to be created to record the outcomes of the drama sessions, and a large poster-sized auction notice. The pupils also produced a number of documents during the course of the drama and these included weekly diary entries showing how different members of the village felt about the process of enclosure, and a variety of 'protest' letters addressed to the squire expressing individual concern about the proposed sale of North Field.

The various resources produced by both teachers and pupils were used to aid the process of learning in the following ways:

(a)   to create an archive history of evidence of one particular enclosure experience that could be used by Alan in helping pupils understand the nature of evidence, and in particular how documents come into being;

(b)   to assist the development of the drama - sometimes a document was used to set up a problem, at other times to illustrate the response to an event;

(c)   in the case of the diary, to act as a reminder to the puils of the previous week's lesson.

The imaginary village of Blockney is based on the example used by Nichol in his text book which was being used by the class.

THE DRAMA SESSIONS

Both classes had two 40 minute history lessons per week. For a period of six weeks one of these lessons was devoted to the drama and the other to a 'straight' history lesson in which Alan took up issues raised in the drama session or used the time to develop further the factual background to enclosure. Prior to each drama session Alan briefed Ray on what he had done in the previous history session. Some of the drama sessions were taken in a drama studio, the rest in the history room.

Session One

We had been able to arrange for both classes to meet together in the drama studio for this session and we were joined by Kevin Katner, Head of Drama, who took an interest in the project and was able to join us on one or two occasions. We introduced the pupils to the idea of using some drama in the forthcoming history topic. The pupils then worked in two class-sized groups and were asked to allocate amongst themselves a number of pieces of card on which were written village occupational roles such as labourer, yeoman, servant, carpenter etc. The pupils were left on their own to decide on the allocation of roles whilst the three teachers acted as advisers to explain any occupational term not understood by the pupils. By the end of the first session the pupils had chosen a role for themselves and, using the large prepared map of Blockney, the pupils began to decide whereabouts in the village they lived.

The purpose of starting both classes together was to establish a distinct starting point to a project in history that would be rather different for the pupils. This lesson illustrates one commonly used way of starting drama through the use of occupational roles. Other ways of starting are, of course possible, such as the use of a story beginning, or a document.

Session Two (the lessons which follow chart the work of just one class).

This session was led by Ray who had prepared copies of an imaginary Vestry Rate book listing the expenditure incurred by the village constable and overseer in 1740. The room was arranged as if for a public meeting and Ray asked for two volunteers who would be prepared to take on the roles of constable and overseer. Ray took on the role of vestry chairman and read through each item adding comments which invited response from the villagers;

Vestry Chairman: <u>Well Mr. Overseer I see from the accounts that you seem to have spent all of 17p on shoes for the Jude boy. Was it really necessary to buy him new shoes, surely he could have had the left-offs of another boy?</u>

Both pupils who had volunteered for the role of constable and overseer made a response to the Chairman's questions and during the 20 minutes that followed various villagers began to identify with the past year's happenings and invent circumstances that fitted the rate book entries. When he came to the end of the expenditure review, the Chairman announced that very little money was left to meet future needs and that perhaps money could be raised by selling off one of the open fields in the village. If this field were to be enclosed far more money could be raised as the land would be more productive. The idea was left in abeyance for a week so that villagers would have time to consider the suggestion.

There had been two aims in mind for this session: the first was to help the pupils further develop their villager roles by giving them a sense of living in a village which had a history of happenings over the previous year; and the other aim was to introduce a problem that would affect everyone.

The purpose of the vestry document was to create a focus for discussion in role. Each villager could choose whether to take an active or spectator role and in fact about half the class spoke as if they were villagers. This enabled the gradual building of a sense of a community with a history. The role of the teacher as vestry chairman was crucial in supporting those who took the first tentative steps in speaking and in building from the villagers' responses a background to a village community and the relationships amongst individuals. During the following week Alan elaborated on the Blockney map by getting pupils to mark in where they lived and worked. In this way the map became a useful 'memory' for the class.

Session Three

This took place in the drama studio and was team taught by Kevin and Ray who took respectively the roles of an ambitious squire from a neighbouring village who had heard rumours about the possible sale of a field in Blockney, and his land surveyor.

The pupils were invited to watch a play and the two teachers met in role and walked around an imaginary field whilst discussing the pros and cons of buying it. From time to time they 'met' some of the villagers whom they drew into conversation by making enquiries about the village and the likely views of people should the field be purchased and enclosed by a new owner. This gave the villagers an opportunity to express their opinions on the matter. At the end of the session Kevin and Ray came out of role and all the villagers were given time to consider their reactions to the proposals made by the squire for the development of the land.

Kevin and Ray were building this session on the work done by Alan during the week on the farming and technology changes that came about in the eighteenth century. The view put forward in role represented the case advanced in favour of change and 'progress'. The challenge for the villagers was to think about the other side of the case and the effect enclosure would have upon those who lost their rights on the open field.

The session began with the villagers taking a spectator role so that the two teachers could feed in information in role. Once this had been established they drew into the play various villagers, who later on told other villagers about the two strangers. Claire's diary entry reflects one villager's view on the events of this session.

Session Four

This session was used to give the pupils an opportunity to argue through the cases for and against enclosure. Alan had done some work on the processes involved before enclosure could be undertaken and it was decided to set up a public hearing before an enclosure commissioner. Alan took this role whilst Ray kept his role of land surveyor representing the squire.

The pupils were given ten minutes to consider their views and the large map of Blockney and a plan showing how the squire proposed to develop North Field were both put on display. For the hearing the pupils sat round in a large circle and the commissioner began by calling on the surveyor to put the squire's case for enclosure. The case that he presented stressed the advantages of enclosure from a farming point of view but deliberately paid scant regard to the plight of villagers who would lose their land. In their statements the villagers took up this point and one villager who described himself as a 'gentleman' said he would like to buy the field and promised to safeguard the interest of the villagers. This move by the pupil created a useful tension between those villagers who liked the idea of working for the squire, those who supported the gentleman, and others who wanted things to remain as they were. Thus the commissioner had three sets of ideas to consider by the end of the session.

It was useful to have two adults in role - one taking a neutral stance and the other biased in favour of enclosure. However if Alan had been on his own it would have been possible (as in most classes) for a pupil to have taken on the role of squire's man. In such a case a pupil could be given time to prepare, perhaps in writing, the case for the squire and this could have been read aloud. Alternatively, a more confident pupil could have arranged the case using a few notes.

Session Five

An important part of this project was the work done by Alan in his history lessons. This article focusses on the drama sessions, but these would not have been possible without Alan's work in history. Sometimes he used these sessions to build up factual background, whilst at other times he encouraged pupils to consider with evidence how far the happenings at Blockney were typical of eighteenth century enclosure and also the extent to which real eighteenth century villagers would have reacted as the Blockney villagers did. The shape of the drama was determined week by week by what Alan saw as history priorities for helping his pupils gain a sound historical understanding of the topic. Had this project been solely one taking place in drama lessons the teaching and learning priorities may have been somewhat different.

For session five Alan wanted his pupils to appreciate the way most commissioners tried to act fairly in dealing with the concerns of all the villagers. He prepared an accurate version of what an enclosure map would look like, although based on the imaginary village of Blockney. This showed not only his award, but related this to the varying quality of land, proposed boundary markings and access roads. He allocated one third of the open field to each of the squire, the gentlemen, and the remaining third to be divided into six pieces and offered for auction. Using the award map he explained his award to the villagers who were then given time to disucss themselves whether or not they would make bids at the forthcoming auction.

Session Six

The spectacle of an auction conjures up visions of a class wildly making higher and higher bids in a totally unrealistic manner. Some thought was given to the best way of handling this lesson, with the result that it was decided to focus less on the auction and more on the way eighteenth century villagers might have raised money to purchase a piece of land. The drama technique used was of a simulation. A fairly complex sequence of activities was planned which allowed the villagers to borrow money from friends or from gold merchants in the City. The factors introduced into the simulation included consideration of interest rates, length of loan and bills of exchange that were signed by both leader and borrower. Some pupils took the role of goldsmiths or wealthy friends who had power to lend a specified amount of money. The rest of the class in role as villagers had to carry out a series of negotiations with a wealthy friend or gold merchant. If a negotiation was successful the borrower was given a bill of exhange. The villagers who ended up with the largest amounts of money were deemed to have bought the six pieces of land on offer at the auction. Whilst the pupils were quite successful at jumping through a series of simulation hoops it is doubtful how far they understood the processes this activity was designed to reveal. This was a good illustration of a piece of simulation that collapsed because it was too complex. The 'collapse' was not brought about by chaos in the classroom - in fact most of the pupils quite enjoyed the work - it was a collapse of any real and thoughtful decision making by the pupils. They were simply following a set of rules with varying degrees of success, but little understanding of the situation the simulation was designed to represent. There is always a danger in trying to build too many reality factors into a piece of drama - in this case, gold merchants, bills of exchange, interest rates and the financial complexities of an eighteenth century money market. Alan had not had time to do any preparatory work with the class so the ideas introduced in the simulation were new to them. On reflection it would have been better to have simplified the whole process by giving each villager a certain amount of capital and then letting the potential buyers discover how much money they could borrow from other villagers.

Some Reflections on the Project

The nature of learning through drama has certain crucial differences from other methods of learning. Drama moves at life rate and at a far slower pace than that set by the text book. It is concerned with particulars - with life in the village, at this particular time, and with a set of people facing in their own particular way a specific problem. By contrast the text book offers a highly generalised and compressed picture of the past which is viewed with hindsight.

This has a number of implications for the history teacher who is entertaining the idea of using drama methods. It is a good learning tool for exploring a small and specific area of the past in depth. It is not efficient for providing broad surveys of the past. In his history lessons Alan showed how it was possible to place the 'small world' of the drama against a wider background by getting his pupils to consider how far their village of Blockney was typical of other villages facing enclosure. Certainly drama raises a number of historical questions ranging from the purely factual ones, which can be researched outside the drama sessions, to deeper questions concerning the social and cultural values of the past. When, as in this project, drama is being used as a tool for learning history, it is of prime importance for the teacher to define carefully which areas of learning can be enhanced through drama and, of equal importance, which ones can best be achieved through other means.

A TUDOR FAYRE, SUMMER 1588

Jo Lawrie, Advisory Teacher, Wiltshire LEA.

It is a fine summer day in the Year of our Lord, 1588. Groups of local people wend their various ways from their own villages, through the Berkshire countryside to their destination - Littlecote House.

At first, these bands of travellers do not appear remarkable. They walk with measured step and many are deep in conversation, discussing the state of the roads or a recent court case when the brewer was charged with watering down the ale. They also escape notice since the natural hues of their garments merge with the earthy tones of the landscape. But, on closer inspection, there can be perceived an air of suppressed excitement. There are two reasons for this. It is the day of the annual midsummer celebration and fayre which has been anticipated for many weeks. Indeed, many are burdened with goods to sell or exchange. But above all, this year the fayre takes place against a background of danger: the threat of the Spaniard.

After walking through the stables, the groups come together in a walled garden in the grounds of Littlecote. After exchanging greetings, everyone begins to set up the stalls ready for the fayre. There are leather purses, quill pens, pottery and jewellery for sale. As well as pomanders and bunches of herbs, there are remedies against the plague on offer, too. If anyone is hungry or thirsty there are oatcakes, gingerbread, apples, sweetmeats, all to be washed down with good ale. Soon there is a whirl of activity as the bargaining begins. Mingling among the crowds the gentry are instantly distinguished by their splendid costume. It is at this point that a cut-purse steals from one of these fine folk. After an exciting chase the thief is caught and taken away to be put in the stocks.

A diversion is created by the arrival of some itinerant players who perform a traditional mummers' play and involve the audience in other jollifications. After further hectic buying and selling the pedlars and stall holders pack away their wares and lunch begins. The gentry sit at a long table eating fine food, prepared according to old receipts, whereas the commonalty sit in groups on the grass, producing their own 'vittels' out of a cloth or basket.

There is much sport with jesters and acrobats performing amid the crowds. Then some musicians play and sing and there is a rendering of <u>Greensleeves</u>. At this point many of the gentry rise to grace the occasion with a dance upon the sward. They are all familiar with the strains of <u>The Earl of Essex</u> measure and begin that stately dance as the music swells. This is followed by <u>Jenny Pluck Pears</u> in which some of the commonalty also join. Whilst the dancing is in full swing a horseman rides into the walled garden at great speed. He has an urgent message for all gathered there. He reads it out, then bids them all to return home with great haste:

'My Lords my ladies good gentle folk, I pray you on this fair day hearken to my wordes of great import. Come hither all. Whilft ye do make merrie here abroad at Littlecote our very land is threatened by the Spanifh fleete that even now doth sail up the Channel west of Plymouth.

In name of Queen and countrie our bold sailors do prepare to meet the foe. Of neceffitie I approach this companie assembled in sport and feafting upon the swarde, for if ye will not see this peaceful land of ours defaced by men from Spayne i' God's nam return to your own villages for safe keepinge and there await for further news from our bold navie. Pray for their good fortune in this battle. Take heed all and God save the Queen'.

Anno 1588

This was the format of a History through Drama Day held in the summer of 1988. It was a deliberately simple format because most of the 250 teachers and pupils involved were new to this approach. However, it was very effective in providing an opportunity for role-playing. Each teacher and pupil had selected a role. Having practised it beforehand, they then tried to stay in this role for the whole time they were at Littlecote, which required considerable concentration. Each school had received a handout to help with the language of the period so that from time to time the odd 'fie', 'forsooth' or 'get ye hence' would be discernible, as an authentic touch.

Background research

The role-playing was also made more effective by researching the role beforehand and finding out about the character's work and way of life and by deciding on personal details such as age and family. Each person dressing in role, using an authentic-looking fabric and style of dress, can help role-playing. There were exercises for the pupils in distinguishing different types of fabric and in comparing Tudor type fabrics with modern ones so that wool, velvet or linen-effect fabrics in subtle colours would be recognised as realistic-looking. There were meetings for parents, to explain this and to suggest cheap sources of fabric - e.g. the reverse side of some old curtains from a jumble sale. A handout gave examples of 1588 styles and showed how the right shape and one or two distinctive details could help. There was a centrally located reference display of quick, simple yet effective costumes and examples of authentic looking accessories such as leather purses, jewellery, shoes and hats. Alongside the costumes were reproductions of Tudor portraits and paintings by Breughel, which had been used as evidence.

Thus role-playing was the main drama technique, with the introduction of unexpected incidents like the cut-purse extending it and allowing for more improvisation. Equally valuable were the history content and the skills and concepts developed in preparing for the drama day itself. Nearly a term's topic work preceded the event. There was coverage of the Armada story itself but concentration was on everyday life leading up to the History through Drama Day. Many of the children had the chance to examine artefacts such as a leather tankard, a horn book and a seal. They did an observational drawing and filled in a record sheet about each object. Some were able to see such objects in context by visiting a Tudor stately home before the final day.

They looked at contemporary portraits not only to find out about costume but also about everyday life: eg. there is a wealth of detail in the paintings of Breughel which they were able to use and communicate at the drama event. Pupils also extracted information from history books, using primary and secondary evidence. They listened to music and learned songs and dances of the period, which added considerably to the authenticity of the day and must have invited comparisons between then and now. Such a variety of sources could only emphasise the nature and value of historical evidence.

In conclusion, may I make a plea for the importance of accurate and authentic historical detail in all aspects of a History through Drama event? If the costume, the accessories, the food, the music and the entertainment are of the period, then this can only complement the historic venue and enrich the drama and role-playing.

BIBLIOGRAPHY

This is a necessarily selective list of publications to guide teachers into further reading. The emphasis is on authors who deal with the implications of practical work in the classroom.

TEACHING HISTORY - GENERAL

Blyth, J.E., (1984), <u>Place and Time with Children 5 - 9</u>, Croom Helm.
"   "   (1988), <u>History 5 - 9</u>, Hodder and Stoughton.
"   "   (1989, new ed.), <u>History in Primary Schools</u>, Open University Press.

DES, (1985), <u>History in the Primary and Secondary Years: An HMI View</u>, HMSO.

DES, (1988), <u>History from 5 to 16: Curriculum Matters 11, an HMI series</u>, HMSO.

Greater Manchester Primary Contact, Special Issue No. 6, (1986), <u>History and the Primary School</u>, Ed. Fairbrother, R.

Lawrie, J., (Ed.), (1987), <u>History-based Topic Work</u>, Wilts.C.C. (Includes section on History through Drama, pp.115-36).

Mays, P., (1985), <u>Teaching Children through the Environment</u>, Hodder and Stoughton.

West, J., (1986), <u>History 7 - 13</u>, Dulston Press.

See also articles in <u>Teaching History</u>, the quarterly journal of the Historical Association. The Appendix of Blyth (1989) gives a list of articles for 1980-7.

TEACHING DRAMA - GENERAL

Davis, G., (1983), <u>Practical Primary Drama</u>, Heinemann.

Linnell, R., (1982), <u>Approaching Classroom Drama</u>, Arnold.

Morgan, N., and Saxon, J., (1987), <u>Teaching Drama</u>, Hutchinson.

Neelands, J., (1984), <u>Making Sense of Drama</u>, Heinemann.

Nixon, J., (1987), <u>Teaching Drama</u>, Macmillan.

O'Neill, C., and Lambert, A., (1982), <u>Drama Structures</u>, Hutchinson.

O'Neill, et al, (1976), <u>Drama Guidelines</u>, Heinemann.

HISTORY THROUGH DRAMA

GENERAL

Barlow, D., and Isenberg, D., (Nov. 1970), 'The use of drama in history teaching', T. Hist., No. 4, pp.303-8.

Fairclough, J., and Redsell, P., (1985), Living History – reconstructing the past with children, Historic Buildings and Monuments Commission.

Fines, J., and Verrier, R., (1974), The Drama of History, New University Education.

Little, V., (June 1983), 'What is Historical Imagination?' T. Hist., No. 36, pp.27-32.

Little, V., (Aut. 1983), 'History through Drama with top juniors', T. Hist., Vol. 11, No. 2, pp.12-18.

May, T., and Williams, S., (Oct. 1987), 'Empathy – a case of Apathy?', T. Hist., No. 49, pp.11-16.

SPECIALIST CENTRES

(Dec. 1981), 'Dramatic Approaches to Museum Education', JEM, No.2, pp.30-3.

Clarke Hall, Wakefield:

Cruickshank, M., 'Home-made history', TES, 17 Oct., 1986, p.29.
Parkin P., 'Tyke time lord', The Guardian, 16 Dec. 1985.

English Heritage:

Anderson, C., (1987), 'A recipe for the past – organising a living history activity', Remnants, No. 3, pp.17-19.
See also the references in Mike Corbishley's contribution, pp. 51-4.

National Trust:

Tinniswood, A., (1986), 'Re-creation, recreation or creation', Resources for Education, No. 10, The National Trust.

EXAMPLES OF SCHOOLS-BASED WORK

Day, R., 'History through Drama: it's more than cowboys and indians', IN, D'Arcy, P., et al, What's Going On? Boynton Cook.

Fines, J., and Nichol, J., (Feb. 1986), 'Domesday Book - past and present', T. Hist., No. 44, pp.5-9.

Hampshire Education, (1988), Drama across the Curriculum: Living History at Netley Abbey. INSET Open Learning Unit; video and notes describing a project involving special and mainstream schools. From Portsmouth Teachers' Resource Centre, Sundridge Close, Portsmouth, PO6 3JL.

Katner, K., et al, (1988), 'The role of drama in the teaching and learning of history', S.E. Hants Drama Centre.

King, J., et al, (Ap. 1988), 'The Big Push: active learning in the humanities with third year pupils', T. Hist., No. 51, pp.15-19.

Marshall, C., (Aug. 1986), 'Off with his head?', Junior Ed., pp.26-7.

Rhodes, J., (1984/5), 'The Battle of Neville's Cross', The Historian, No. 5, p.11.

Schools Council, (1977), Talking, Writing and Learning 8-13, Working Paper 59, Evans/Methuen, section on pp.52-60, '...life in a Saxon community'.

Tucker, J., (Aut. 1985), 'Drama and the Moral Dimension', 2D - Drama and Dance, pp.30-53.

Verrier, R., (Aut. 1981), 'Using historical documents with children', London Drama, Vol. 6, No. 5, pp.17-19.

EXAMPLES OF OUR OWN PROJECTS FEATURED IN THIS PAMPHLET ARE PUBLISHED AS FOLLOWS:

Saxons and Normans at Britford:

Woodhouse, J., (Ap. 1985), 'History through Drama', Junior Ed, p.11.

Tudor Court Leet:

Wilson, V., and Woodhouse, J., (Oct., 1987), 'History through Drama: an enactive approach to learning', Ed. 3-13, Vol. 15, No. 3, pp.33-6.

Woodhouse, J., and Wilson, V., (1988), 'The Tudor Court Leet of 1566', IN Blyth, J., (1988), History 5 - 9, Hodder and Stoughton, pp.58-60.

A video recording of this project entitled Court Leet is available for hire or purchase from Wessex Educational Television, King Alfred's College, Winchester, SO22 4NR.

Iron Age at Danebury:

Woodhouse, J., and Wilson, V., (Ap. 1988), 'Celebrating the solstice – a History through Drama teaching project on the Iron Age', T. Hist., No 51, pp.10-14.
Woodhouse, J., and Wilson, V., 'Danebury solstice...', IN Blyth, J., (1989), History in Primary Schools, Open University Press, pp.33-6.

USEFUL ADDRESSES

National contacts:

Archaeology Alive, University of Manchester, Oxford Rd., Manchester, M13 9PL.

Archaeology in Education, Dept of Archaeology and Prehistory, University of Sheffield, Sheffield, S10 2TN

English Heritage Education Service, 15/17 Great Marlborough St, London, W1V 1AF.

Historical Association, 59A Kennington Park Rd, London, SE11 4JH.

National Trust, PO Box 30, Beckenham, Kent, BR3 4TZ.

Primary History Association, details from Karen Svanso (Secretary), St John's Wood CP School, Knutsford, Cheshire, WA16 8PA.

Unicorn Theatre for Children, 679 Newport St., London, WC2.

Young Archaeologists' Club, United House, Piccadilly, York, YO1 1PQ.

Local contacts:

It is impossible to give a national survey of the relevant support services. We recommend that teachers identify their local contacts from the following general list:

LEA: county advisors and advisory teachers for history/humanities and drama;

Teacher training institutions;

Museum education service;

Local library and record office;

Local history society and branches of specialist societies, eg. the Sealed Knot.

Rangers/education service officers attached to Country Parks or similar, administered by local Recreation Depts.

In many areas local companies may well be willing to provide items which could be of use to a project. For an example of the types of contacts which could be made, see Fairclough and Redsell, op. cit., Appendix B, p.27.

For more specific information on the Hampshire area we can be contacted at La Sainte Union College of Higher Education, The Avenue, Southampton, SO9 5HB. Tel: (0703) 228761.